THE APOLOGY OF THE CHURCH OF ENGLAND

John Jewel

Bishop of Salisbury.
CaselL & Company, Ltd:
London, Paris, New York & Melbourne
1888

Contents

THE APOLOGY OF THE CHURCH OF ENGLAND

BY

JOHN JEWEL

INTRODUCTION

The great interest of Jewel's "Apology" lies in the fact that it was written in Latin to be read throughout Europe as the answer of the Reformed Church of England, at the beginning of Queen Elizabeth's reign, to those who said that the Reformation set up a new Church. Its argument was that the English Church Reformers were going back to the old Church, not setting up a new; and this Jewel proposed to show by looking back to the first centuries of Christianity. Innovation was imputed; and an Apology originally meant a pleading to rebut an imputation. So, even as late as 1796, there was a book called "An Apology for the Bible," meaning its defence against those who questioned its authority. This Latin book of Jewel's, *Apologia Ecclesiae Anglicanae*--written in Latin because it was not addressed to England only--was first published in 1562, and translated into English by the mother of Francis Bacon, whose edition appeared in 1564. That is the translation given in this volume. The book has since had six or seven other translators, but Lady Ann Bacon's translation was that which presented it in Queen Elizabeth's time to English readers, and it had the advantage of revision by the Queen's Archbishop of Canterbury, her coadjutor in the establishment of the Reformed Church of England, Matthew Parker. It was published, with no name of author or translator on the title-page, as "An Apologie or answere in defence of the Churche of Englande, with a briefe and plaine declaration of the true Religion professed or used in the same." The book was prefaced by a letter, "To the right honorable learned and vertuous Ladie, A. B." [Ann Bacon] "M. C. wisheth from God grace, honoure, and felicitie," where M. C. signifies Matthew Cantuar, Matthew Parker, Archbishop of Canterbury, whom Lady Ann Bacon had made her judge, and whose judgment, the letter says, her book had singularly pleased.

Lady Ann Bacon was the second daughter of Sir Anthony Cooke, who was tutor to King Edward VI. Sir Anthony gave to his five daughters a most liberal education. His eldest daughter, Mildred, married Sir William Cecil, afterwards Lord Burleigh, while Ann became the second wife of the Lord Keeper, Sir Nicholas Bacon. Their father had made Mildred and Ann two of the most learned women in England.

John Jewel was forty years old when he wrote the "Apology." He was born in Devonshire in 1522, on the 24th of May, at the village of Buden, near Ilfracombe. He studied at Oxford, where he became tutor and preacher, graduated as B.D. in 1551, and was presented to the rectory of Sunningwell. At the accession of Queen Mary he bowed to the royal authority, but he was a warm friend and disciple of Peter Martyr, who had come to England in 1547, at the invitation of Edward VI., to take the chair of Divinity at Oxford. On the accession of Queen Mary, Peter Martyr (who was born at Florence in 1500, and whose family name was Vermigli) returned to Strasburg, and went thence to Zurich, where he died in 1562. Jewel, repenting of his assent to the new sovereign's authority in matters of religion, followed his friend Peter Martyr across the water, and became vice-master of a college at Strasburg. Upon the accession of Elizabeth, in 1588, Jewel came back, and he was one of the sixteen Protestants appointed by the Queen to dispute before her with a like number of Catholics.

In 1559 John Jewel was appointed a commissioner for securing, in the West of England, conformity with the newly-arranged Church service, and he had to see that the Queen's orders were obeyed in the churches of his native county. Before the end of the same year he was consecrated Bishop of Salisbury. He was most zealous in performance of all duties of his charge. To his good offices young Richard Hooker owed his opportunity of training for the service of the Church. Among Jewel's writings, this Apology or Defence of the Church of England was the most important; but he worked incessantly, and shortened his life by limiting himself to four hours of sleep, taken between midnight and four in the morning. Bishop Jewel died on the 21st of September, 1571, before he had reached the age of fifty.

H. M.

AN APOLOGY, OR ANSWER, IN DEFENCE OF THE CHURCH OF ENGLAND

With a Brief and Plain Declaration of the True Religion Professed and Used in the Same.

PART I

It hath been an old complaint, even from the first time of the patriarchs and Prophets, and confirmed by the writings and testimonies of every age, that the truth wandereth here and there as a stranger in the world, and doth readily find enemies and slanderers amongst those that know her not. Albeit perchance this may seem unto some a thing hard to be believed, I mean to such as have scant well and narrowly taken heed thereunto, specially seeing all mankind of nature's very motion without a teacher doth covet the truth of their own accord; and seeing our Saviour Christ Himself, when He was on earth, would be called the Truth, as by a name most fit to express all His Divine power; yet we, which have been exercised in the Holy Scriptures, and which have both read and seen what hath happened to all godly men commonly at all times; what to the Prophets, to the Apostles, to the holy martyrs, and what to Christ Himself; with what rebukes, revilings, and despites they were continually vexed whiles they here lived, and that only for the truth's sake: we, I say, do see that this is not only no new thing, or hard to be believed, but that it is a thing already received, and commonly used from age to age. Nay, truly, this might seem much rather a marvel, and beyond all belief, if the devil, who is the father of lies, and enemy to all truth, would now upon a sudden change his nature, and hope that truth might otherwise be suppressed than by belying it; or that he would begin to establish his own kingdom by using now any other practices than the same which he hath ever used from the beginning. For since any man's remembrance we can scant find one time, either when religion did first grow, or when it was settled, or when it did afresh spring up again, wherein truth and innocency were not by all unworthy means, and most despitefully intreated. Doubtless the devil well seeth, that so long as truth is in good safety, himself cannot be safe, nor yet maintain his own estate.

For, letting pass the ancient patriarchs and Prophets, who, as we have said, had no part of their life free from contumelies and slanders, we know there were certain in times past which said and commonly preached, that the old ancient Jews (of whom we make no doubt but they were the worshippers of the only and true God) did worship either a sow, or an ass, in God's stead, and that all the same religion was nothing else but a sacrilege, and a plain contempt of all godliness. We know also that the Son of God, our Saviour Jesu Christ, when He taught the truth, was counted a juggler and an enchanter, a Samaritan, Beelzebub, a deceiver of the people, a drunkard, and a glutton. Again, who wotteth not what words were spoken against St. Paul, the most earnest and vehement preacher and maintainer of the truth? sometime that he was a seditious and busy man, a raiser of tumults, a causer of rebellion; sometime again, that he was an heretic; sometime, that he was mad; sometime, that only upon strife and stomach he was both a blasphemer of God's law, and a despiser of the fathers' ordinances. Further, who knoweth not how St. Stephen, after he had thoroughly and sincerely embraced the truth, and began frankly and stoutly to preach and set forth the same, as he ought to do, was immediately called to answer for his life, as one that had wickedly uttered disdainful and heinous words against the law, against Moses, against the temple, and against God? Or who is ignorant that in times past there were some which reproved the Holy Scripts of falsehood, saying they contained things both contrary and quite one against other; and how that the Apostles of Christ did severally disagree between themselves, and that St. Paul did vary from them all? And, not to make rehearsal of all, for that were an endless labour, who knoweth not after what sort our fathers were railed upon in times past, which first began to acknowledge and profess the Name of Christ? how they made private conspiracies, devised secret counsels against the commonwealth, and that end made early and privy meetings in the dark, killed young babes, fed themselves with men's flesh, and, like savage and brute beasts, did drink their blood? in conclusion, how that, after they had put out the candles, they committed adultery between themselves, and without regard wrought incest one with another: that brethren lay with their sisters, sons with their mothers, without any reverence of nature or kin, without shame without difference; and that they were wicked men without all care of religion, and without any opinion of God, being the very enemies of mankind, unworthy to be suffered in the world, and unworthy of life?

All these things were spoken in those days against the people of God, against Christ Jesu, against Paul, against Stephen, and against all them, whosoever they were, which at the first beginning embraced the truth of the Gospel, and were contented to be called by the name of Christians, which was then a hateful name among the common people. And although the things which they said were not true, yet the devil thought it should be sufficient for him, if at the least he could bring it so to pass as they might be believed for true, and that the Christians might be brought into a common hatred of everybody, and have their death and destruction sought of all sorts. Hereupon kings and princes, being led then by such persuasions, killed all the Prophets of God, letting none escape. Esay with a saw, Jeremy with stones, Daniel with lions, Amos with an iron bar, Paul with the sword, and Christ upon the cross; and condemned all Christians to imprisonments, to torments, to the pikes, to be thrown down headlong from rocks and steep places, to be cast to wild beasts, and to be burnt: and made great fires of their quick bodies, for the only purpose to give light by night, and for a very scorn and mocking stock; and did count them no better than the vilest filth, the offscourings and laughing games of the whole world. Thus, as ye see, have the authors and professors of the truth ever been intreated.

Wherefore, we ought to bear it the more quietly, which have taken upon us to profess the Gospel of Christ, if we for the same cause be handled after the same sort; and if we, as our forefathers were long ago, be likewise at this day tormented, and baited with railings, with spiteful dealings, and with lies; and that for no desert of our own, but only because we teach and acknowledge the truth.

They cry out upon us at this present everywhere, that we are all heretics, and have forsaken the faith, and have with new persuasions and wicked learning utterly dissolved the concord of the Church; that we renew, and, as it were, fetch again from hell the old and many a day condemned heresies; that we sow abroad new sects, and such broils as never yearst were heard of: also that we are already divided into contrary parts and opinions, and could yet by no means agree well among ourselves; that we be cursed creatures, and, like the giants, do war against God Himself, and live clean without any regard or worshipping of God; that we despise all good deeds; that we use no discipline of virtue, no laws, no customs; that we esteem neither right, nor order, nor equity, nor justice; that we give the bridle to all naughtiness, and provoke the people to all licentiousness and lust; that we labour and seek to overthrow the state of monarchies and kingdoms, and to bring all things under the rule of the rash inconstant people and unlearned multitude; that we have seditiously fallen from the Catholic Church, and by a wicked schism and division have shaken the whole world, and troubled the common peace and universal quiet of the Church; and that, as Dathan and Abiram conspired in times past against Moses and Aaron, even so we at this day have renounced the Bishop of Rome without any cause reasonable; that we set nought by the authority of the ancient fathers and councils of old time; that we have rashly and presumptuously disannulled the old ceremonies, which have been well allowed by our fathers and forefathers many hundred years past, both by good customs, and also in ages of more purity; and that we have by our own private head, without the authority of any sacred and general council, brought new traditions into the Church: and have done all these things not for religion's sake, but only upon a desire of contention and strife; but that they for their part have changed no manner of thing, but have held and kept still such a number of years to this very day all things as they were delivered from the Apostles and well approved by the most ancient fathers.

And that this matter should not seem to be done but upon privy slander, and to be tossed to and fro in a corner, only to spite us, there have been besides wilily procured by the Bishop of Rome certain persons of eloquence enough, and not unlearned neither, which should put their help to this cause, now almost despaired of, and should polish and set forth the same, both in books, and with long tales to the end that, when the matter was trimly and eloquently handled, ignorant and unskilful persons might suspect there was some great thing in it. Indeed they perceived that their own cause did everywhere go to wrack; that their sleights were now espied, and less esteemed; and that their helps did daily fail them; and that their matter stood altogether in great need of a cunning spokesman.

Now as for those things which by them have been laid against us, in part they be manifestly false, and condemned so by their own judgments which spake them; partly again, though they be as false, too, indeed, yet bear they a certain show and colour of truth, so as the reader (if he take not good heed) may easily be tripped and brought into error by them, specially when their fine and cunning tale is added thereunto. And part of them be of such sort as we ought not to shun them as crimes or faults, but to acknowledge and profess them as things well done, and upon very good reason.

For shortly to say the truth, these folk falsely accuse and slander all our doings; yea the same things which they themselves cannot deny but to be rightly and orderly done; and for malice do so misconstrue and deprave all our sayings and doings, as though it were impossible that anything could be rightly spoken or done by us. They should more plainly and sincerely have gone to work if they would have dealt truly. But now they neither truly, nor sincerely, nor yet Christianly, but darkly and craftily charge and batter us with lies, and do abuse the blindness and fondness of the people, together with the ignorance of princes, to cause us to be hated and the truth to be suppressed. This, lo, ye, is the power of darkness, and of men which lean more to the amazed wondering of the rude multitude and to darkness than they do to truth and light; and as St. Hierom saith, which do openly gainsay the truth, closing up their eyes, and will not see for the nonce.

But we give thanks to the most good and mighty God, that such is our cause, whereagainst (when they would fainest) they were able to utter no despite, but the same which might as well be wrested against the holy fathers, against the Prophets, against the Apostles, against Peter, against Paul, and against Christ Himself.

Now, therefore, if it be lawful for these folks to be eloquent and fine- tongued in speaking evil, surely it becometh not us in our cause, being so very good, to be dumb in answering truly. For men to be careless what is spoken by them and their own matter, be it never so falsely and slanderously spoken (especially when it is such that the majesty of God and the cause of religion may thereby be damaged), is the part doubtless of dissolute and wretchless persons, and of them which wickedly wink at the injuries done unto the Name of God. For although other wrongs, yea oftentimes great, may be borne and dissembled of a mild and Christian man, yet he that goeth smoothly away, and dissembleth the matter when he is noted of heresy, Ruffinus was wont to deny that man to be a Christian. We therefore will do the same thing, which all laws, which nature's own voice doth command to be done, and which Christ Himself did in like case, when He was checked and reviled: to the intent we may put off from us these men's slanderous accusations, and may defend soberly and truly our own cause and innocency. For Christ verily, when the Pharisees charged Him with sorcery, as one that had some familiar spirits, and wrought many things by their help: "I," said He, "have not the devil, but do glorify my Father: but it is you that have dishonoured me, and put me to rebuke and shame." And St. Paul, when Festus the lieutenant scorned him as a madman: "I," said he, "most dear Festus, am not mad, as thou thinkest, but I speak the words of truth and soberness." And the ancient Christians, when they were slandered to the people for mankillers, for adulterers, for committers of incest, for disturbers of the commonweals, and did perceive that by such slanderous accusations the religion which they professed might be brought in question, namely, if they should seem to hold their peace, and in manner to confess the fault; lest this might hinder the free course of the Gospel, they made orations, they put up supplications, and made means to emperors and princes, that they might defend themselves and their fellows in open audience.

But we truly, seeing that so many thousands of our brethren in these last twenty years have borne witness unto the truth, in the midst of most painful torments that could be devised; and when princes, desirous to restrain the Gospel, sought many ways, but prevailed nothing; and that now almost the whole world doth begin to open their eyes to behold the light; we take it that our cause hath already been sufficiently declared and defended, and think it not needful to make many words, seeing the matter saith enough for itself. For if the popes would, or else if they could weigh with their own selves the whole matter, and also the beginnings and proceedings of our religion, how in a manner all their travail hath come to nought, nobody driving it forward; and how on the other side, our cause, against the will of emperors from the beginning, against the wills of so many kings, in spite of the popes, and almost maugre the head of all men, hath taken increase, and by little and little spread over into all countries, and is come at length even into kings' courts and palaces; these same things, methinketh, might be tokens great enough to them, that God Himself doth strongly fight in our quarrel, and doth from heaven laugh at their enterprises; and that the force of truth is such, as neither man's power, nor yet hell-gates are able to root it out. For they be not all mad at this day, so many free cities, so many kings, so many princes, which have fallen away from the seat of Rome, and have rather joined themselves to the Gospel of Christ.

And although the popes had never hitherunto leisure to consider diligently and earnestly of these matters, or though some other cares do now let them, and diverse ways pull them, or though they count these to be but common and trifling studies, and nothing to appertain to the Pope's worthiness, this maketh not why our matter ought to seem the worse. Or if they perchance will not see that which they see indeed, but rather will withstand the known truth, ought we therefore by-and-by to be accounted heretics because we obey not their will and pleasure? If so be, that Pope Pius were the man (we say not, which he would so gladly be called), but if he were indeed a man that either would account us for his brethren, or at least would take us to be men, he would first diligently have examined our reasons, and would have seen what might be said with us, what against us; and would not in his bull, whereby he lately pretended a council, so rashly have condemned so great a part of the world, so many learned and godly men, so many commonwealths, so many kings, and so many princes, only upon his own blind prejudices and fore- determinations--and that without hearing of them speak or without showing cause why.

But because he hath already so noted us openly, lest by holding our peace we should seem to grant a fault, and specially because we can by no means have audience in the public assembly of the general council, wherein he would no creature should have power to give his voice or to declare his opinion, except he be sworn, and straitly bound to maintain his authority (for we have had good experience hereof in the last conference at the council at Trident; where the ambassadors and divines of the princes of Germany, and of the free cities, were quite shut out from their company. Neither can we yet forget, how Julius the Third, above ten years past, provided warily by his writ that none of our sort should be suffered to speak in the council, except that there were some, peradventure, that would recant and change his opinion): for this cause chiefly we thought it good to yield up an account of our faith in writing, and truly and openly to make answer to those things wherewith we have been openly charged; to the end the world may see the parts and foundations of that doctrine, in the behalf whereof so many good men have little regarded their own lives; and that all men may understand what manner of people they be, and what opinion they have of God and of religion, whom the Bishop of Rome, before they were called to tell their tale, hath condemned for heretics, without any good consideration, without any example, and utterly without law or right, only because he heard tell that they did dissent from him and his in some point of religion.

And although St. Hierom would have nobody to be patient when he is suspected of heresy, yet we will deal herein neither bitterly nor brablingly; nor yet be carried away with anger and heat; though he ought to be reckoned neither bitter nor brabler that speaketh the truth. We willingly leave this kind of eloquence to our adversaries, who, whatsoever they say against us, be it never so shrewdly or despitefully said, yet think it is said modestly and comely enough, and care nothing whether it be true or false. We need none of these shifts which do maintain the truth.

Further, if we do show it plainly that God's holy Gospel, the ancient bishops, and the primitive Church do make on our side, and that we have not without just cause left these men, and rather have returned to the Apostles and old Catholic fathers; and if we shall be found to do the same not colourably or craftily, but in good faith before God, truly, honestly, clearly, and plainly; and if they themselves which fly our doctrine, and would be called

Catholics, shall manifestly see how all these titles of antiquity, whereof they boast so much, are quite shaken out of their hands; and that there is more pith in this our cause than they thought for; we then hope and trust that none of them will be so negligent and careless of his own salvation, but he will at length study and bethink himself to whether part he were best to join him. Undoubtedly, except one will altogether harden his heart and refuse to hear, he shall not repent him to give good heed to this our Defence, and to mark well what we say, and how truly and justly it agreeth with Christian religion.

For where they call us heretics, it is a crime so heinous, that unless it may be seen, unless it may be felt, and in manner may be holden with hands and fingers, it ought not lightly to be judged or believed, when it is laid to the charge of any Christian man. For heresy is a forsaking of salvation, a renouncing of God's grace, a departing from the body and spirit of Christ. But this was ever an old and solemn property with them and their forefathers; if any did complain of their errors and faults, and desired to have true religion restored, straightway to condemn such ones for heretics, as men new-fangled and factious. Christ for no other cause was called a Samaritan, but only for that He was thought to have fallen to a certain new religion, and to be the author of a new sect. And Paul the Apostle of Christ was called before the judges to make answer to a matter of heresy; and therefore he said: "According to this way which they call heresy I do worship the God of my fathers, believing all things which be written in the law and in the Prophets."

Shortly to speak. This universal religion which Christian men profess at this day was called first of the heathen people a sect and heresy. With these terms did they always fill princes' ears, to the intent when they had once hated us with a predetermined opinion, and had counted all that we said to be faction and heresy, they might be so led away from the truth and right understanding of the cause. But the more sore and outrageous a crime heresy is, the more it ought to be proved by plain and strong arguments, especially in this time, when men begin to give less credit to their words, and to make more diligent search of their doctrine, than they were wont to do. For the people of God are otherwise instructed now than they were in times past, when all the bishops of Rome's sayings were allowed for Gospel, and when all religion did depend only upon their authority. Nowadays the Holy Scripture is abroad, the writings of the Apostles and Prophets are in print, whereby all truth and Catholic doctrine may be proved, and all heresy may be disproved and confuted.

Sithence, then, they bring forth none of these for themselves, and call us nevertheless heretics, which have neither fallen from Christ, nor from the Apostles, nor yet from the Prophets, this is an injurious and a very spiteful dealing. With this sword did Christ put off the devil when He was tempted of him: with these weapons ought all presumption, which doth advance itself against God, to be overthrown and conquered. "For all Scripture," saith St. Paul, "that cometh by the inspiration of God, is profitable to teach, to confute, to instruct, and to reprove, that the man of God may be perfect, and thoroughly framed to every good work." Thus did the holy fathers always fight against the heretics with none other force than with the Holy Scriptures. St. Augustine, when he disputed against Petilian, a heretic of the Donatists: "Let not these words," quoth he, "be heard between us, 'I say, or you say:' let us rather speak in this wise: 'Thus saith the Lord.' There let us seek the Church: there let us boult out our cause." Likewise St. Hierom: "All those things," saith he, "which without the testimony of the Scriptures are holden as delivered from the Apostles, be thoroughly smitten down by the sword of God's word." St. Ambrose also, to Gratian the emperor: "Let the Scripture," saith he, "be asked the question, let the prophets be asked, and let Christ be asked." For at that time made the Catholic fathers and bishops no doubt but that our religion might be proved out of the Holy Scriptures. Neither were they ever so hardy as to take any for a heretic whose error they could not evidently and apparently reprove by the self-same Scriptures. And we verily do make answer on this wise, as St. Paul did: "According to this way which they call heresy we do worship God, and the Father of our Lord Jesus Christ; and do allow all things which have been written either in the law or in the Prophets," or in the Apostles' works.

Wherefore, if we be heretics, and they (as they would fain be called) be Catholics, why do they not, as they see the fathers, which were Catholic men, have always done? Why do they not convince and master us by the Divine Scriptures? Why do they not call us again to be tried by them? Why do they not lay before us how we have gone away from Christ, from the Prophets, from the Apostles, and from the holy fathers? Why stick they to do it? Why are they afraid of it? It is God's cause. Why are they doubtful to commit it to the trial of God's word? If we be heretics, which refer all our controversies unto the Holy Scriptures, and report us to the self-same words which we know were sealed by God Himself, and in comparison of them set little by all other things, whatsoever may be devised by men, how shall we say to these folk, I pray you what manner of men be they, and how is it meet to call them, which fear the judgment of the Holy Scriptures--that is to say, the judgment of God Himself--and do prefer before them their own dreams and full cold inventions; and, to maintain their own traditions, have defaced and corrupted, now these many hundred years, the ordinances of Christ and of the Apostles?

Men say that Sophocles, the tragical poet, when in his old days he was by his own sons accused before the judges for a doting and sottish man, as one that fondly wasted his own substance, and seemed to need a governor to see unto him; to the intent he might clear himself of the fault, he came into the place of judgment; and when he had rehearsed before them his tragedy called *OEdipus Coloneus*, which he had written at the very time of his accusation, marvellous exactly and cunningly, did of himself ask the judges whether they thought any sottish or doting man could do the like piece of work.

In like manner, because these men take us to be mad, and appeach us for heretics, as men which have nothing to do, neither with Christ, nor with the Church of God, we have judged it should be to good purpose, and not unprofitable, if we do openly and frankly set forth our faith wherein we stand, and show all that confidence which we have in Christ Jesu; to the intent all men may see what is our judgment of every part of Christian religion, and may resolve with themselves, whether the faith which they shall see confirmed by the words of Christ, by the writings of the Apostles, by the testimonies of the Catholic fathers, and by the examples of many ages, be but a certain rage of furious and mad men, and a conspiracy of heretics. This therefore is our belief.

PART II

We believe that there is one certain nature and Divine power, which we call God: and that the same is divided into three equal Persons--into the Father, into the Son, and into the Holy Ghost; and that They all be of one power, of one majesty, of one eternity, of one Godhead, and of one substance. And although these three Persons be so divided, that neither the Father is the Son, nor the Son is the Holy Ghost, or the Father; yet, nevertheless, we believe that there is but one very God, and that the same one God hath created heaven, and earth, and all things contained under heaven.

We believe that Jesus Christ, the only Son of the eternal Father (as long before it was determined before all beginnings), when the fulness of time was come, did take of that blessed and pure Virgin both flesh and all the nature of man, that He might declare to the world the secret and hid will of His Father; which will had been laid up from before all ages and generations; and that He might full finish in His human body the mystery of our redemption; and might fasten our sins to the cross, and also that handwriting which was made against us.

We believe that for our sakes He died, and was buried, descended into hell, the third day by the power of His Godhead returned to life, and rose again; and that the fortieth day after His resurrection, whiles His disciples beheld and looked upon Him He ascended into heaven to fulfil all things, and did place in majesty and glory the self-same body wherewith He was born, wherein He lived on earth, wherein He was jested at, wherein He had suffered most painful torments and cruel kind of death, wherein He rose again, and wherein He ascended to the right hand of the Father, "above all rule, above all power, all force, all dominion, and above every name that is named, not only in this world, but also in the world to come:" and that there He now sitteth, and shall sit, till all things be full perfected. And although the Majesty and Godhead of Christ be everywhere abundantly dispersed, yet we believe that his body, as St. Augustine saith, must needs be still in one place; and that Christ hath given majesty unto His body, but yet hath not taken away from it the nature of a body; and that we must not so affirm Christ to be God that we deny Him to be man: and, as the Martyr Vigilius saith, that Christ hath left us as touching His human nature, but hath not left us as touching His Divine nature; and that the same Christ, though He be absent from us concerning His manhood, yet is ever present with us concerning his Godhead.

From that place also we believe that Christ shall come again to execute that general judgment, as well of them whom He shall then find alive in the body as of them that be already dead.

We believe that the Holy Ghost, who is the third person in the Holy Trinity, is very God: not made, not created, not begotten, but proceeding from both the Father and the Son, by a certain mean unknown unto men, and unspeakable; and that it is His property to mollify and soften the hardness of man's heart when He is once received thereinto, either by the wholesome preaching of the Gospel, or by any other way: that he doth give men light, and guide them unto the knowledge of God; to all way of truth; to newness of the whole life; and to everlasting hope of salvation.

* * * * *

We believe that there is one Church of God, and that the same is not shut up (as in times past among the Jews) into some one corner or kingdom, but that it is catholic and universal, and dispersed throughout the whole world. So that there is now no nation which may truly complain that they be shut forth, and may not be one of the Church and people of God: and that this Church is the kingdom, the body, and the spouse of Christ; and that Christ alone is the Prince of this kingdom; that Christ alone is the Head of this Body; and that Christ alone is the Bridegroom of this spouse.

Furthermore, we believe that there be divers degrees of ministers in the Church; whereof some be deacons, some priests, some bishops; to whom is committed the office to instruct the people, and the whole charge and setting forth of religion. Yet notwithstanding, we say that there neither is, nor can be any one man, which may have the whole superiority in this universal state: for that Christ is ever present to assist His Church, and needeth not any man to supply His room, as His only heir to all His substance: and that there can be no one mortal creature, which is able to comprehend or conceive in his mind the universal Church, that is to wit, all the parts of the world, much less able rightly and duly to put them in order, and to govern them rightly and duly. For all the Apostles, as Cyprian saith, were of like power among themselves, and the rest were the same that Peter was, and that it said indifferently to them all, "feed ye;" indifferently to them all, "go into the whole world;" indifferently to them all, "teach ye the Gospel." And (as Hierom saith) all bishops wheresoever they be, be they at Rome, be they at Eugubium, be they at Constantinople, be they at Rhegium, be all of like pre-eminence, and of like priesthood. And, as Cyprian saith, there is but one bishopric, and a piece thereof is perfectly and wholly holden of every particular bishop. And according to the judgment of the Nicene Council, we say, that the Bishop of Rome hath no more jurisdiction over the Church of God than the rest of the patriarchs, either of Alexandria, or of Antiochia have. And as for the Bishop of Rome, who now calleth all matters before himself alone, except he do his duty as he ought to do, except he minister the Sacraments, except he instruct the people, except he warn them and teach them, we say that he ought not of right once to be called a bishop, or so much as an elder. For a bishop, as saith Augustine, is a name of labour, and not of honour: because he will have that man understand himself to be no bishop, which will seek to have pre- eminence, and not to profit others. And that neither the Pope, nor any other worldly creature can no more be head of the whole Church, or a bishop over all, than he can be the bridegroom, the light, the salvation, and life of the Church. For the privileges and names belong only to Christ, and be properly and only fit for him alone. And that no Bishop of Rome did ever suffer himself to be called by such a proud name before Phocas the emperor's time, who, as we know, by killing his own sovereign

Maurice the emperor, did by a traitorous villainy aspire to the empire about the six hundredth and thirteenth year after Christ was born. Also the Council of Carthage did circumspectly provide, that no bishop should be called the highest bishop or chief priest. And therefore, sithence the Bishop of Rome will nowadays so be called, and challengeth unto himself an authority that is none of his; besides that he doth plainly contrary to the ancient councils, and contrary to the old fathers; we believe that he doth give unto himself, as it is written by his own companion Gregory, a presumptuous, a profane, a sacrilegious, and an antichristian name: that he is also the king of pride, that he is Lucifer, which preferreth himself before his brethren: that he hath forsaken the faith, and is the forerunner of Antichrist.

Further we say, that the minister ought lawfully, duly, and orderly to be preferred to that office of the Church of God, and that no man hath power to wrest himself into the holy ministry at his own pleasure and list. Wherefore these persons do us the greater wrong, which have nothing so common in their mouths, as that we do nothing orderly and comely, but all things troublesomely and without order; and that we allow every man to be a priest, to be a teacher, and to be an interpreter of the Scriptures.

Moreover, we say that Christ hath given to His ministers power to bind, to loose, to open, to shut. And that the office of loosing consisteth in this point: that the minister should either offer by the preaching of the Gospel the merits of Christ and full pardon, to such as have lowly and contrite hearts, and do unfeignedly repent themselves, pronouncing unto the same a sure and undoubted forgiveness of their sins, and hope of everlasting salvation: or else that the same minister, when any have offended their brothers' minds with a great offence, with a notable and open fault, whereby they have, as it were, banished and made themselves strangers from the common fellowship, and from the body of Christ; then after perfect amendment of such persons, doth reconcile them, and bring them home again, and restore them to the company and unity of the faithful. We say also, that the minister doth execute the authority of binding and shutting, as often as he shutteth up the gate of the kingdom of heaven against the unbelieving and stubborn persons, denouncing unto them God's vengeance, and everlasting punishment: or else, when he doth quite shut them out from the bosom of the Church by open excommunication. Out of doubt, what sentence soever the minister of God shall give in this sort, God Himself doth so well allow of it, that whatsoever here in earth by their means is loosed and bound, God Himself will loose and bind, and confirm the same in heaven. And touching the keys, wherewith they may either shut or open the kingdom of heaven, we with Chrysostom say, "They be the knowledge of the Scriptures:" with Tertullian we say, "They be the interpretation of the law:" and with Eusebius, we call them "The Word of God." Moreover, that Christ's disciples did receive this authority, not that they should hear the private confessions of the people and listen to their whisperings, as the common massing-priests do everywhere nowadays, and do it so, as though in that one point lay all the virtue and use of the keys: but to the end they should go, they should teach, they should publish abroad the Gospel, and be unto the believing a sweet savour of life unto life, and unto the unbelieving and unfaithful a savour of death unto death; and that the minds of godly persons being brought low by the remorse of their former life and errors, after they once began to look up unto the light of the Gospel, and believe in Christ, might be opened with the Word of God, even as a door is opened with a key. Contrariwise, that the wicked and wilful folk, and such as would not believe, nor return into the right way, should be left still as fast locked, and shut up, and, as St. Paul saith, "wax worse and worse." This take we to be the meaning of the keys; and that after this sort men's consciences either be opened or shut. We say, that the priest indeed is a judge in this case, but yet hath no manner of right to challenge an authority, or power, as saith Ambrose. And therefore our Saviour Jesu Christ, to reprove the negligence of the Scribes and Pharisees in teaching, did with these words rebuke them, saying: "Woe be unto you Scribes and Pharisees, which have taken away the keys of knowledge, and have shut up the kingdom of heaven before men." Seeing then the key whereby the way and entry to the kingdom of God is opened unto us, is the word of the Gospel, and the expounding of the law and Scriptures; we say plainly, where the same word is not there is not the key. And seeing one manner of word is given to all, and one only key belongeth to all, we say, that there is but one only power of all ministers; as concerning opening and shutting. And as touching the Bishop of Rome, for all his parasites flatteringly sing these words in his ears, "To thee will I give the keys of the kingdom of heaven" (as though those keys were fit for him alone, and for nobody else), except he go so to work, as men's consciences may be made pliant, and be subdued to the Word of God, we deny that he doth either open, or shut, or hath the keys at all. And although he taught and instructed the people (as would God he might once truly do, and persuade himself it were at the least some piece of his duty), yet we think his key to be never a whit better, or of greater force than other men's. For who hath severed him from the rest? Who hath taught him more cunningly to open, or better to absolve than his brethren?

We say that matrimony is holy and honourable in all sorts and states of persons, in the patriarchs, in the Prophets, in the Apostles, in holy martyrs, in the ministers of the Church, and in bishops; and that it is an honest and lawful thing (as Chrysostom saith) for a man, living in matrimony, to take upon him therewith the dignity of a bishop. And as Sozomenus saith of Spiridion; and as Nazianzen saith of his own father, that a good and diligent bishop doth serve in the ministry never the worse for that he is married, but rather the better, and with more ableness to do good. Further, we say, that the same law which by constraint taketh away this liberty from men, and compelleth them against their wills to live single, is the doctrine of devils, as Paul saith: and, that, ever sithence the time of this law, a wonderful uncleanness of life and manners in God's ministers, and sundry horrible enormities have followed, as the Bishop of Augusta, as Faber, as Abbas Panormitanus, as Latomus, as the tripartite work, which is annexed to the second tome of the councils, and other champions of the Pope's band, yea, and as the matter itself, and all histories do confess. For it was rightly said by Pius the Second, Bishop of Rome, "that he saw many causes why wives should be taken away from priests, but that he saw many more, and more weighty causes why they ought to be restored them again."

* * * * *

We receive and embrace all the canonical Scriptures, both of the Old and New Testament, giving thanks to our God, who hath raised up unto us that light which we might ever have before our eyes, lest either by the subtlety of man, or by the snares of the devil, we should be carried away to errors and lies. Also that these be the heavenly voices, whereby God hath opened unto us His will: and that only in them man's heart can have settled rest; that in them be abundantly and fully comprehended all things, whatsoever be needful for our salvation, as Origen, Augustine, Chrysostom, and Cyrillus have taught: that they be the very might and strength of God to attain to salvation: that they be the foundations of the Prophets and Apostles, whereupon is built the Church of God: that they be the very sure and infallible rule, whereby may be tried, whether the Church do stagger, or err, and whereunto all ecclesiastical doctrine ought to be called to account: and that against these Scriptures neither law, nor ordinance, nor any custom ought to be heard: no, though Paul his own self, or an angel from heaven, should come and teach the contrary.

* * * * *

Moreover, we allow the Sacraments of the Church, that is to say, certain holy signs and ceremonies, which Christ would we should use, that by them He might set before our eyes the mysteries of our salvation, and might more strongly confirm our faith which we have in His blood, and might seal His grace in our hearts. And these Sacraments, together with Tertullian, Origen, Ambrose, Hierom, Chrysostom, Basil, Dionysius, and other Catholic fathers, do we call figures, signs, marks or badges, prints, copies, forms, seals, signets, similitudes, patterns, representations, remembrances and memories. And we make no doubt, together with the same doctors, to say, that these be certain visible words, seals of righteousness, tokens of grace: and do expressly pronounce, that in the Lord's Supper there is truly given unto the believing the body and blood of the Lord, the flesh of the Son of God, which quickeneth our souls, the meat that cometh from above, the food of immortality, grace, truth, and life, and the Supper to be the communion of the body and blood of Christ; by the partaking whereof we be revived, we be strengthened, and be fed unto immortality; and whereby we are joined, united, and incorporate unto Christ, that we may abide in Him, and He in us.

Besides, we acknowledge there be two Sacraments, which, we judge, properly ought to be called by this name; that is to say, Baptism and the Sacrament of thanksgiving. For thus many we say were delivered and sanctified by Christ, and well allowed of the old fathers, Ambrose and Augustine.

* * * * *

We say that Baptism is a Sacrament of the remission of sins, and of that washing, which we have in the blood of Christ; and that no person which will profess Christ's Name ought to be restrained or kept back therefrom; no, not the very babes of Christians; forsomuch as they be born in sin, and do pertain unto the people of God.

We say, that Eucharistia, that is to say the Supper of the Lord, is a Sacrament; that is to wit, an evident token of the body and blood of Christ, wherein is set, as it were, before our eyes, the death of Christ and His resurrection, and what act soever He did whilst He was in His mortal body: to the end we may give Him thanks for His death, and for our deliverance: and that, by the often receiving of this Sacrament, we may daily renew the remembrance of that matter, to the intent we, being fed with the

[true] body and blood of Christ, may be brought into the hope of the resurrection and of everlasting life, and may most assuredly believe that the body and blood of Christ doth in like manner feed our souls, as bread and wine doth feed our bodies. To this banquet we think the people of God ought to be earnestly bidden, that they may all communicate among themselves, and openly declare and testify both the godly society which is among them, and also the hope which they have in Christ Jesu. For this cause if there had been any which would be but a looker-on, and abstain from the Holy Communion, him did the old fathers and bishops of Rome in the primitive Church, before private mass came up, excommunicate as a wicked person and as a pagan. Neither was there any Christian at that time which did communicate alone, whiles other looked on. For so did Calixtus in times past decree, "that after the consecration was finished, all should communicate, except they had rather stand without the church-doors; because thus (saith he) did the Apostles appoint, and the same the holy Church of Rome keepeth still."

Moreover, when the people cometh to the Holy Communion, the Sacrament ought to be given them in both kinds: for so both Christ hath commanded, and the Apostles in every place have ordained, and all the ancient fathers and Catholic bishops have followed the same. And whoso doth contrary to this, he (as Gelasius saith) committeth sacrilege. And therefore we say, that our adversaries at this day, who having violently thrust out, and quite forbidden the Holy Communion, do, without the word of God, without the authority of any ancient council, without any Catholic father, without any example of the primitive Church, yea, and without reason also, defend and maintain their private masses, and the mangling of the Sacraments, and do this not only against the plain express commandment and bidding of Christ, but also against all antiquity, do wickedly therein, and are very Church robbers.

We affirm that bread and wine are holy and heavenly mysteries of the body and blood of Christ, and that by them Christ Himself, being the true bread of eternal life, is so presently given unto us as that by faith we verily receive his body and his blood. Yet say we not this so, as though we thought that the nature and substance of the bread and wine is clearly changed and goeth to nothing: as many have dreamed in these later times, which yet could never agree among themselves, of this their dream. For that was not Christ's meaning, that the wheaten bread should lay apart his own nature, and receive a certain new divinity: but that he might rather change us, and (to use Theophylact's words) might transform us into His body. For what can be said more plainly, than that which Ambrose saith: "Bread and wine remain still the same they were before, and yet are changed into another thing:" or, that which Gelasius saith: "The substance of the bread, or the nature of the wine, ceaseth not so to be:" or, that which Theodoret saith: "After the consecration the mystical signs do not cast off their own proper nature; for they remain still on their former substance, form, and kind:" or that which Augustine saith: "That which ye see is the bread and cup, for so our eyes tell us: but that which your faith requireth to be taught, is this: the bread is the body of Christ, and the cup is His blood:" or that which Origen saith: "The bread which is sanctified by the Word of God, as touching the material substance thereof, goeth into the belly, and is cast out into the privy:" or that which Christ Himself said, not only after the blessing of the cup, but after he had ministered the communion: "I will drink no more of this fruit of the vine." It is well known that the fruit of the vine is wine, and not blood.

And in speaking thus, we mean not to abase the Lord's Supper, that it is but a cold ceremony only, and nothing to be wrought therein (as many falsely slander us we teach). For we affirm, that Christ doth truly and presently give His own self in His Sacraments; in Baptism, that we may put Him on; and in His Supper, that we may eat Him by faith and spirit, and may have everlasting life by His Cross and blood. And we say not, this is done slightly and coldly, but effectually and truly. For although we do not touch the body of Christ with teeth and mouth, yet we hold Him fast, and eat Him by faith, by understanding, and by the Spirit. And it is no vain faith which doth comprehend Christ: and that is not received with cold devotion, that is received with understanding, with faith, and with spirit. For Christ Himself altogether is so offered and given us in these mysteries, that we may certainly know we be flesh of His flesh, and bone of His bones; and that Christ "continueth in us, and we in Him." And therefore in celebrating these mysteries, the people are to good purpose exhorted before they come to receive the Holy Communion, to lift up their hearts, and to direct their minds to heavenward: because He is there, by whom we must be full fed, and live. Cyril saith, when we come to receive these mysteries, all gross imaginations must quite be banished. The Council of Nice, as is alleged by some in Greek, plainly forbiddeth us to be basely affectioned, or bent toward the bread and wine, which are set before us. And, as Chrysostom very aptly writeth, we say, "that the body of Christ is the dead carcase, and we ourselves must be the eagles," meaning thereby that we must fly high, if we will come unto the body of Christ. "For this table," as Chrysostom saith, "is a table of eagles, and not of jays." Cyprian also, "This bread," saith he, "is the food of the soul, and not the meat of the belly." And Augustine, "How shall I hold Him," saith he, "which is absent? How shall I reach my hand up to heaven, to lay hold upon Him that sitteth there?" He answereth, "Reach hither thy faith, and then thou hast laid hold on Him."

We cannot also away in our churches with the shows, and sales, and buying and selling of masses, nor the carrying about and worshipping of bread: nor such other idolatrous and blasphemous fondness: which none of them can prove that Christ or His Apostles did ever ordain, or left unto us. And we justly blame the bishops of Rome, who, without the word of God, without the authority of the holy fathers, without any example of antiquity, after a new guise, do not only set before the people the sacramental bread to be worshipped as God, but do also carry about the same upon an ambling horse, whithersoever themselves journey, as in old times the Persians' fire, and the relics of the goddess Isis, were solemnly carried about in procession: and have brought the Sacraments of Christ to be used now as a stage play and a solemn sight: to the end, that men's eyes should be fed with nothing else but with mad gazings and foolish gauds, in the self-same matter, wherein the death of Christ ought diligently to be beaten into our hearts, and wherein also the mysteries of our redemption ought with all holiness and reverence to be executed.

Besides, where they say, and sometimes do persuade fools, that they are able by their masses to distribute and apply unto men's commodity all the merits of Christ's death, yea, although many times the parties think nothing of the matter, and understand full little what is done, this is a mockery, an heathenish fancy, and a very toy. For it is our faith that applieth the death and cross of Christ to our benefit, and not the act of the massing priest. "Faith had in the Sacraments," saith Augustine, "doth justify, and not the Sacraments." And Origen saith, "Christ is the Priest, the Propitiation, and Sacrifice: which Propitiation cometh to every one by means of faith." So that by this reckoning, we say that the Sacraments of Christ without faith do not once profit these that be alive; a great deal less do they profit those that be dead.

And as for their brags they are wont to make of their purgatory, though we know it is not a thing so very late risen amongst them, yet is it no better than a blockish and an old wives' device. Augustine, indeed, sometime saith, there is such a certain place: sometime he denieth not, but there may be such a one; sometime he doubteth; sometime again he utterly denieth it to be, and thinketh that men are therein deceived by a certain natural good will they bear their friends departed. But yet of this one error hath there grown up such a harvest of these mass-mongers, the masses being sold abroad commonly in every corner, the temples of God became shops to get money: and silly souls were persuaded that nothing was more necessary to be bought. Indeed, there was nothing more gainful for these men to sell.

As touching the multitude of vain and superfluous ceremonies, we know that Augustine did grievously complain of them in his own time: and therefore have we cut off a great number of them, because we know that men's consciences were cumbered about them, and the churches of God overladen with them.

Nevertheless we keep still, and esteem, not only those ceremonies which we are sure were delivered us from the Apostles, but some others too besides, which we thought might be suffered without hurt to the Church of God: because that we had a desire that all things in the holy congregation might (as St. Paul commandeth) "be done with comeliness and in good order." But as for all those things which we saw were either very superstitious, or wholly unprofitable, or noisome, or mockeries, or contrary to the Holy Scriptures, or else unseemly for honest or discreet folks, as there be an infinite number nowadays where papistry is used; these, I say, we have utterly refused without all manner exception, because we would not have the right worshipping of God any longer denied with such follies.

We make our prayers in that tongue which all our people, as meet is, may understand, to the end they may (as Paul counselleth us) take common commodity by common prayer, even as all the holy fathers and Catholic bishops, both in the Old and New Testament, did used to pray themselves, and taught the people to pray too, lest, as Augustine saith, "like parrots and ousels we should seem to speak that we understand not."

Neither have we any other mediator and intercessor, by whom we may have access to God the Father, than Jesus Christ, in whose only Name all things are obtained at His Father's hand. But it is a shameful part, and full of infidelity, that we see every whore used in the churches of our adversaries, not only in that they will have innumerable sorts of mediators, and that utterly without the authority of God's word (so that, as Jeremy saith, "The saints be now as many in number, or rather above the number of the cities;" and poor men cannot tell to which saint it were best to turn them first; and though there be so many as they cannot be told, yet every one of them hath his peculiar duty and office assigned unto him of these folks, what thing they ought to ask, what to give, and what to bring to pass): but besides this also, in that they do not only wickedly, but also shamefully, call upon the Blessed Virgin, Christ's mother, to have her remember that she is the mother, and to command her Son, and to use a mother's authority over Him.

We say also, that every person is born in sin, and leadeth his life in sin: that nobody is able truly to say his heart is clean: that the most righteous person is but an unprofitable servant: that the law of God is perfect, and requireth of us perfect and full obedience: that we are able by no means to fulfil that law in this worldly life: that there is no one mortal creature which can be justified by his own deserts in God's sight: and therefore that our only succour and refuge is to fly to the mercy of our Father by Jesu Christ, and assuredly to persuade our minds that He is the obtainer of forgiveness for our sins; and that by His blood all our spots of sin be washed clean: that He hath pacified and set at one, all things by the blood of His Cross: that He by the same one only Sacrifice, which He once offered upon the Cross, hath brought to effect and fulfilled all things, and that for that cause He said, when He gave up the ghost, "It is finished," as though He would signify, that the price and ransom was now full paid for the sin of all mankind. If there be any, then, that think this Sacrifice not sufficient, let them go, in God's Name, and seek another that is better. We, verily, because we know this to be the only Sacrifice, are well content with it alone and look for none other: and, forasmuch as it was to be offered but once, we command it not to be renewed again: and because it was full and perfect in all points and parts, we do not ordain in place thereof any continual succession of offerings.

Besides, though we say, we have no meed at all by our own works and deeds, but appoint all the means of our salvation to be in Christ alone, yet say we not, that for this cause men ought to live loosely and dissolutely: nor that it is enough for a Christian to be baptised only and to believe: as though there were nothing else required at his hand. For true faith is lively, and can in no wise be idle.

Thus therefore teach we the people, that God hath called us, not to follow riot and wantonness, but, as St. Paul saith, "unto good works, to walk in them:" that God hath plucked us out "from the power of darkness, to the end that we should serve the living God;" to cut away all the remnants of sin, and "to work our salvation in fear and trembling:" that it may appear, how that the Spirit of sanctification is in our bodies, and that Christ Himself doth dwell in our hearts.

To conclude, we believe, that this our self-same flesh wherein we live, although it die, and come to dust, yet at the last day it shall return again to life, by the means of Christ's Spirit which dwelleth in us: and that then verily, whatsoever we suffer here in the meanwhile for His sake, Christ will wipe away all tears and lamentation from our eyes: and that we through Him shall enjoy everlasting life, and shall for ever be with Him in glory. So be it.

PART III

Behold these are the horrible heresies, for the which, a good part of the world is at this day condemned by the Bishop of Rome; and yet were never heard to plead their cause. He should have commenced his suit rather against Christ, against the Apostles, and against the holy fathers. For these things did not only proceed from them, but were also appointed by them: except perhaps these men will say (as I think they will indeed), that Christ never instituted the Holy Communion to be divided amongst the faithful; or that Christ's Apostles and the ancient fathers said private masses in every corner of the temples, now ten, now twenty together in one day: or that Christ and His Apostles banished all the common people from the Sacrament of His blood: or that the thing, which they themselves do at this day everywhere, and do it so as they condemn him for a heretic which doth otherwise, is not called of Gelasius, their own doctor, plain sacrilege: or that these be not the very words of Ambrose, Augustine, Gelasius, Theodoret, Chrysostom, and Origen: "The bread and wine in the Sacraments remain still the same they were before:" "The thing which is seen upon the Holy Table is bread;" "There ceaseth not to be still the substance of bread, and nature of wine;" "The substance and nature of bread are not changed;" "The self-same bread, as touching the material substance, goeth into the belly, and is cast out into the privy:" or that Christ, the Apostles, and holy fathers prayed not in that tongue which the people might understand: or that Christ hath not performed all things by that one offering which He once offered: or that the same sacrifice was unperfect, and so now we have need of another. All these things must they of necessity say, unless perchance they had rather say thus, that "all law and right is locked up in the treasury of the Pope's breast," and that, as once one of his soothing pages and claw-backs did not stick to say, "The Pope is able to dispense against the Apostles;" against a council, and against the canons and rules of the Apostles: and that he is not bound to stand neither to the examples, nor to the ordinances, nor to the laws of Christ. We, for our part, have learned these things of Christ, of the Apostles, of the devout fathers: and do sincerely, with good faith, teach the people of God the same. Which thing is the only cause why we at this day are called heretics of the chief prelates (no doubt) of religion.

O immortal God! hath Christ Himself, then, the Apostles, and so many fathers all at once gone astray? Were then Origen, Ambrose, Augustine, Chrysostom, Gelasius, Theodoret, forsakers of the Catholic faith? was so notable a consent of so many ancient bishops and learned men nothing else but a conspiracy of heretics? or is that now condemned in us, which was then commended in them? or is the thing now, by alteration only of men's affections, suddenly become schismatic, which in them was counted Catholic? or shall that which in times past was true, now by-and-by, because it liketh not these men, be judged false? let them then bring forth another Gospel, and let them show the causes why these things, which so long have openly been observed and well-allowed in the Church of God, ought now in the end to be called in again. We know well enough that the same word which was opened by Christ, and spread abroad by the Apostles, is sufficient both, our salvation and all truth, to uphold and maintain; and also to confound all manner of heresy. By that word only do we condemn all sorts of the old heretics, whom these men say we have called out of hell again. As for the Arians, the Eutychians, the Marcionites, the Ebionites, the Valentinians, the Carpocratians, the Tatians, the Novatians, and shortly all them which have a wicked opinion, either of God the Father, or of Christ, or of the Holy Ghost, or of any other point of Christian religion, forsomuch as they be confuted by the Gospel of Christ, we plainly pronounce them for detestable and castaway persons, and defy them even unto the devil. Neither do we leave them so, but we also severely and straitly hold them in by lawful and politic punishments, if they fortune to break out anywhere, and bewray themselves.

Indeed, we grant that certain new and very strange sects, as the Anabaptists, Libertines, Menonians, and Zuenckfeldians, have been stirring in the world ever since the Gospel did first spring. But the world seeth now right well, thanks be given to our God, that we neither have bred, nor taught, nor kept up these monsters. In good fellowship, I pray thee, whosoever thou be, read our books: they are to be sold in every place. What hath there ever been written by any of our company which might plainly bear with the madness of any of those heretics. Nay, I say unto you, there is no country this day so free from their pestilent infections, as they be, wherein the Gospel is freely and commonly taught. So that if they weigh the very matter with earnest and upright advisement, this thing is a great argument, that this same is the very truth of the Gospel of Christ, which we do teach. For lightly neither is cockle wont to grow without the wheat, nor yet the chaff without the corn. For from the very Apostles' times, who knoweth not how many heresies did rise up even together so soon, as the Gospel was first spread abroad? Who ever had heard tell of Simon, Menander, Saturninus, Basilides, Carpocrates, Cerinthus, Ebion, Valentinus, Secundus, Marcosius, Colorbasius, Heracleo, Lucianus, and Severus, before the Apostles were sent abroad? But why stand we reckoning up these? Epiphanius rehearseth up fourscore sundry heresies; and Augustine many more, which sprang up even together with the Gospel? What then? Was the Gospel therefore not the Gospel, because heresies sprang up withal? or was Christ therefore not Christ? And yet, as we said, doth not this great crop and heap of heresies grow up amongst us, which do openly, abroad, and frankly teach the Gospel. These poisons take their beginnings, their increasings, and strength, amongst our adversaries, in blindness and in darkness, amongst whom truth is with cruelty and tyranny kept under, and cannot be heard but in corners and secret meetings. But let them make a proof: let them give the Gospel free passage: let the truth of Jesu Christ give his clear light, and stretch forth His bright beams into all parts: and then shall they forthwith see how all these shadows straight will vanish and pass away at the light of the Gospel, even as the thick mist of the night consumeth at the sight of the sun. For whilst these men sit still, and make merry and do nothing, we continually repress and put back all those heresies which they falsely charge us to nourish and maintain.

Where they say, that we have fallen into sundry sects, and would be called some of us Lutherians, and some of us Zuinglians, and cannot yet well agree among ourselves touching the whole substance of doctrine: what would these men have said, if they had been in the first times of the Apostles and holy fathers, when one said, "I hold of Paul;" another, "I hold of Cephas;" another, "I hold of Apollo;" when Paul did so sharply rebuke Peter; when, upon a falling out, Barnabas departed from Paul; when, as Origen mentioneth, the Christians were divided into so many factions, as that they kept no more but the name of Christians in common among them, being in no manner of thing else like unto Christians; when, as Socrates saith, for their dissensions and sundry sects they were laughed and jested at openly of the people in the common game-plays; when, as Constantine the emperor affirmeth, there were such a number of variances and brawlings in the Church, that it might justly seem a misery far passing all the former miseries; when also Theophilus, Epiphanius, Chrysostom, Augustine, Ruffine, Hierom, being all Christians, being all fathers, being all Catholics, did strive one against another with most bitter and remediless contentions without end; when, as saith Nazianzen, the parts of one body were consumed and wasted one of another; when the east part was divided from the west, only for leavened bread and only for keeping of Easter Day; which were indeed no great matters to be strived for; and when in all councils new creeds and new decrees continually were devised. What would these men (trow ye) have said in those days? which side would they specially then have taken? and which would they then have forsaken? which Gospel would they have believed? whom would they have accounted for heretics, and whom for Catholics? And yet what a stir and revel keep they at this time upon two poor names only of Luther and Zuinglius? Because these two men do not yet fully agree upon some one point, therefore would they needs have us think that both of them were deceived; that neither of them had the Gospel; and that neither of them taught the truth aright.

But, good God, what manner of fellows be these which blame us for disagreeing? And do all they themselves, ween you, agree well together? Is every one of them fully resolved what to follow? Hath there been no strifes, no debates, no quarrels among them at no time? Why then do the Scotists and the Thomists, about that they call *meritum congrui and meritum condigni*, no better agree together? Why agree they no better among themselves concerning original sin in the Blessed Virgin? concerning a solemn vow and a single vow? Why say the canonists, that auricular confession is appointed by the positive law of man: and the schoolmen contrariwise, that it is appointed by the law of God? Why doth Albertus Pighius dissent from Cajetanus? Why doth Thomas dissent from Lombardus, Scotus from Thomas, Occamus from Scotus, Alliacensis [ed. 1564 Alliensis] from Occamus? And why do the Nominals disagree from the Reals? And yet say I nothing of so many diversities of friars and monks; how some of them put a great holiness in eating of fish, and some in eating of herbs; some in wearing of shoes, and some in wearing of sandals; some in going in a linen garment, and some in a woollen; some of them called white, some black; some being shaven broad, and some narrow: some stalking abroad upon pattens, some barefooted; some girt, and some ungirt. They ought, I wiss, to remember, how there be some of their own company which say, that the body of Christ is in His Supper naturally: contrary, other some of the self-same company deny it to be so. Again, that there be other of them, which say, the body of Christ in the Holy Communion "is rent and torn with our teeth:" and some again that deny the same. Some also of them there be, which write that the body of Christ is *quantum* in the Eucharistia; that is to say, hath his perfect quantity in the Sacrament; some other again say nay. That there be others of them which say Christ did consecrate with a certain Divine power: some, that he did the same with His blessing: some again that say, He did it with uttering five solemn chosen words: and some, with rehearsing the same words afterward again. Some will have it, that, when Christ did speak those five words, the material wheaten bread was pointed by this demonstrative pronoun *hoc*: some had rather have, that a certain *vagum individuum*, as they term it, was meant thereby. Again, others there be that say dogs and mice may truly and in very deed eat the body of Christ; and others again there be that steadfastly deny it. There be others, which say, that the very accidents of bread and wine may nourish: others again there be which say, how that the substance of bread doth return again. What need I say more? It were overlong and tedious to reckon up all things. So very uncertain, and full of controversies, is yet the whole form of these men's religion and doctrine, even amongst themselves, from whence it did first spring and begin. For hardly at any time do they well agree between themselves: except it be peradventure as, in times past, the Pharisees and Sadducees; or as Herod and Pilate did accord against Christ.

They were best, therefore, to go and set peace at home rather among their own selves. Of a truth, unity and concord doth best become religion: yet is not unity the sure and certain mark whereby to know the Church of God. For there was the greatest consent that might be amongst them that worshipped the golden calf; and among them which with one voice jointly cried against our Saviour Jesus Christ, "Crucify Him." Neither, because the Corinthians were unquieted with private dissensions: or because Paul did square with Peter, or Barnabas with Paul: or, because the Christians, upon the very beginning of the Gospel, were at mutual discord touching some one matter or other, may we therefore think there was no Church of God amongst them. And as for those persons, whom they upon spite call Zuinglians and Lutherians, in very deed they of both sides be Christians, good friends and brethren. They vary not betwixt themselves upon the principles and foundations of our religion, nor as touching God, nor Christ, nor the Holy Ghost, nor of the means of justification, nor yet everlasting life, but upon one only question, which is neither weighty nor great: neither mistrust we, or make doubt at all, but they will shortly be agreed. And if there be any of them which have other opinion than is meet, we doubt not but ere it be long they will put apart all affections and names of parties, and that God will reveal it unto them: so that by better considering and searching out of the matter, as once it came to pass in the Council of Chalcedon, all causes and seeds of dissension shall be thoroughly plucked up by the root, and be buried, and quite forgotten for ever. Which God grant.

But this is the most grievous and heavy case, that they call us wicked and ungodly men, and say we have thrown away all care of religion. Though this ought not to trouble us much, whilst they themselves that thus have charged us know full well how spiteful and false a saying it is: for Justin the martyr is a witness, how that all Christians were called [Greek text], that is, godless, as soon as the Gospel first began to be published, and the Name of Christ to be openly declared. And when Polycarpus stood to be judged, the people stirred up the president to slay and murder all them which professed the Gospel, with these words, [Greek text], that is to say, "Rid out of the way these wicked and godless creatures." And this was not because it was true that the Christians were godless, but because they would not worship stones and stocks which were then honoured as God. The whole world seeth plainly enough already, what we and ours have endured at these men's hands for religion and our only God's cause. They have thrown us into prison, into water, into fire, and imbrued themselves in our blood: not because we were either adulterers, or robbers, or murderers, but only for that we confessed the Gospel of Jesu Christ, and put our confidence in the living God; and for that we complained too justly and truly (Lord, thou knowest), that they did break the law of God for their own most vain traditions; and that our adversaries were the very foes to the Gospel, and enemies to Christ's Cross, who so wittingly and willingly did obstinately despise God's commandments.

Wherefore, when these men saw they could not rightly find fault with our doctrine, they would needs pick a quarrel and inveigh and rail against our manners, surmising, how that we do condemn all well-doings: that we set open the door to all licentiousness and lust, and lead away the people from all love of virtue. And in very deed, the life of all men, even of the devoutest and most Christian, both is, and evermore hath been, such as one may always find some lack, even in the very best and purest conversation. And such is the inclination of all creatures unto evil, and the readiness of all men to suspect that the things which neither have been done, nor once meant to be done, yet may be easily both heard and credited for true. And like as a small spot is soon espied in the neatest and whitest garment, even so the least stain of dishonesty is easily found out in the purest and sincerest life. Neither take we all them which have at this day embraced the doctrine of the Gospel, to be angels, and to live clearly without any mote or wrinkle; nor yet think we these men either so blind, that if anything may be noted in us, they are not able to perceive the same even through the least crevice: nor so friendly, that they will construe aught to the best: nor yet so honest of nature nor courteous, that they will look back upon themselves, and weigh our fashions by their own. If so be we list to search this matter from the bottom, we know in the very Apostles' times there were Christians, through whom the Name of the Lord was blasphemed and evil spoken of among the Gentiles. Constantius the emperor bewaileth, as it is written in Sozomenus, that many waxed worse after they had fallen to the religion of Christ. And Cyprian, in a lamentable oration, setteth out the corrupt manners in his time: "The wholesome discipline," saith he, "which the Apostles left unto us, hath idleness and long rest now utterly marred: everyone studied to increase his livelihood; and clean forgetting either what they had done before whilst they were under the Apostles, or what they ought continually to do, having received the faith they earnestly laboured to make great their own wealth with an unsatiable desire of covetousness. There is no devout religion," saith he, "in priests, no sound faith in ministers, no charity showed in good works, no form of godliness in their conditions: men are become effeminate, and women's beauty is counterfeited." And before his days, said Tertullian, "O how wretched be we, which are called Christians at this time! for we live as heathens under the Name of Christ." And without reciting of many more writers, Gregory Nazianzen speaketh thus of the pitiful state of his own time: "We," saith he, "are in hatred among the heathen for our own vices' sake; we are also become now a wonder, not only to angels and men, but even to all the ungodly." In this case was the Church of God, when the Gospel first began to shine, and when the fury of tyrants was not as yet cooled, nor the sword taken off from the Christians' necks. Surely it is no new thing that men be but men, although they be called by the name of Christians.

PART IV

But will these men, I pray you, think nothing at all of themselves, while they accuse us so maliciously? And while they have leisure to behold so far off, and see both what is done in Germany and in England, have they either forgotten, or can they not see what is done at Rome? or be they our accusers, whose life is such as no man is able to make mention thereof but with shame and uncomeliness? Our purpose here is, not to take in hand, at this present, to bring to light and open to the world those things which were meet rather to be hid and buried with the workers of them. It beseemeth neither our religion, nor our modesty, nor our shamefastness. But yet he, which giveth commandment that he should be called the "Vicar of Christ," and the "Head of the Church;" who also heareth that such things be done in Rome, who seeth them, who suffereth them (for we will go no further), he can easily consider with himself what manner of things they be. Let him on God's Name call to mind, let him remember that they be of his own canonists, which have taught the people that fornication between single folk is no sin (as though they had fette that doctrine from Mitio in Terence), whose words be: "It is no sin (believe me) for a young man to haunt harlots." Let him remember they be of his own which have decreed, that a priest ought not to be put out of his cure for fornication. Let him remember also how Cardinal Campegius, Albertus Pighius, and others many more of his own, have taught, that the priest which "keepeth a concubine" doth live more holily and chastely than he which hath a "wife in matrimony." I trust he hath not yet forgotten that there be many thousands of common harlots in Rome; and that himself doth gather yearly of the same harlots upon, a thirty thousand ducats, by the way of an annual pension. Neither can he forget, how himself doth maintain openly brothel houses, and by a most filthy lucre doth filthily and lewdly serve his own lust. Were all things then pure and holy in Rome, when "Joan a woman," rather of perfect age than of perfect life, was Pope there, and bare herself as the "head of the Church:" and after that for two whole years in that holy see she had played the naughty pack, at last, going in procession about the city, in the sight of all the cardinals and bishops, fell in travail openly in the streets.

But what need we rehearse concubines and bawds? as for that is now an ordinary and a gainful sin at Rome. For harlots sit there now-a-days, not as they did in times past, without the city walls, and with their faces hid and covered, but they dwell in palaces and fair houses: they stray about in court and market, and that with bare and open face: as who say, they may not only lawfully do it, but ought also to be praised for so doing. What should we say any more of this? Their vicious and abominable life is now thoroughly known to the whole world. Bernard writeth roundly and truly of the Bishop of Rome's house, yea, and of the Bishop of Rome himself. "Thy palace," saith he, "taketh in good men, but it maketh none; naughty persons thrive there, and the good appayre and decay." And whosoever he were which wrote the Tripartite work, annexed to the Council Lateranense, saith thus: "So excessive at this day is the riot, as well in the prelates and bishops as in the clerks and priests, that it is horrible to be told."

But these things be not only grown in ure, and so by custom and continual time well allowed, as all the rest of their doings in manner be, but they are now waxen old and rotten ripe. For who hath not heard what a heinous act Peter Aloisius, Pope Paul the Third's son, committed against Cosmus Cherius, the Bishop of Fanum; what John, Archbishop of Beneventum, the Pope's legate at Venice, wrote in the commendation of a most abominable filthiness: and how he set forth, with most loathsome words and wicked eloquence, the matter which ought not once to proceed out of anybody's mouth! To whose ears hath it not come, that N. Diasius, a Spaniard, being purposely sent from Rome into Germany, so shamefully and devilishly murdered his own brother John Diasius, a most innocent and a most godly man, only because he had embraced the Gospel of Jesu Christ, and would not return again to Rome?

But it may chance to this they will say: These things may sometime happen in the best governed commonwealths, yea, and against the magistrates' wills: and besides, there be good laws made to punish such. I grant it be so: but by what good laws (I would know) have these great mischiefs been punished amongst them? Petrus Aloisius, after he had done that notorious act that I spake of, was always cherished in his father's bosom, Pope Paul the Third, and made his very derling. Diasius, after he had murdered his own brother, was delivered by the Pope's means, to the end he might not be punished by good laws. John Casus, the Archbishop of Beneventum, is yet alive, yea, and liveth at Rome, even in the eyes and sight of the most holy father.

They have put to death infinite numbers of our brethren, only because they believed truly and sincerely in Jesu Christ. But of that great and foul number of harlots, fornicators, adulterers, what one have they at any time (I say not killed, but) either excommunicated, or once attached? Why! voluptuousness, adultery, ribaldry, whoredom, murdering of kin, incest, and others more abominable parts, are not these counted sin at Rome? Or, if they be sin, ought "Christ's vicar, Peter's successor, the most holy father," so lightly and slightly to bear them, as though they were no sin, and that in the city of Rome, and in that principal tower of all holiness?

O holy Scribes and Pharisees, which knew not this kind of holiness! what a Catholic faith is this! Peter did not thus teach at Rome: Paul did not so live at Rome: they did not practise brothelry, which these do openly: they made not a yearly revenue and profit of harlots: they suffered no common adulterers and wicked murderers to go unpunished. They did not receive them into their entire familiarity, into their council, into their household, nor yet into the company of Christian men. These men ought not therefore so unreasonably to triumph against our living. It had been more wisdom for them either first to have proved good their own life before the world, or at least to have cloaked it a little more cunningly. For we do use still the old and ancient laws, and (as much as men may do, in the manners used at these days, all things are so wholly corrupt) we diligently and earnestly put in execution the ecclesiastical discipline: we have not common brothel-houses of strumpets, nor yet flocks of concubines, nor herds of harlot-hunters: neither do we prefer adultery before matrimony: neither do we exercise beastly sensuality: neither do we gather ordinary rents and stipends of stews: nor do we suffer to escape unpunished incest and abominable naughtiness, nor yet such manquellers as the Aloisians, Casians, and Diazians were. For if these things would have pleased us, we needed not to have departed from these men's fellowship, amongst whom such enormities be in their chief pride and price. Neither needed we, for leaving them, to run into the hatred of men, and into most wilful dangers. Paul the Fourth, not many months sithence, had at Rome in prison certain Augustine friars, many bishops, and a great number of other devout men, for religion's sake. He racked them and tormented them: to make them confess, he left no means unassayed. But in the end how many brothels, how many whoremongers, how many adulterers, how many incestuous persons could he find of all those? Our God be thanked, although we be not the men we ought and profess to be, yet, whosoever we be, compare us with these men, and even our own life and innocency will soon prove untrue and condemn their malicious surmises. For we exhort the people to all virtue and well-doing, not only by books and preachings, but also with our examples and behaviour. We also teach that the Gospel is not a boasting or bragging of knowledge, but that it is the law of life, and that a Christian man (as Tertullian saith) "ought not to speak honourably, but ought to live honourably; nor that they be the hearers of the law, but the doers of the law, which are justified before God."

Besides all these matters wherewith they charge us, they are wont also to add this one thing, which they enlarge with all kind of spitefulness: that is, that we be men of trouble, that we pluck the "sword and sceptre out of kings' hands;" that we arm the people: that we overthrow judgment places, destroy the laws, make havoc of possessions, seek to make the people princes, turn all things upside down: and, to be short, that we would have nothing in good frame in a commonwealth. Good Lord, how often have they set on fire princes' hearts with these words, to the end they might quench the light of the Gospel in the very first appearing of it, and might begin to hate the same ere ever they were able to know it, and to the end that every magistrate might think he saw his deadly enemy as often as he saw any of us!

Surely it should exceedingly grieve us to be so maliciously accused of most heinous treason, unless we knew that Christ Himself, the Apostles, and a number of good and Christian men, were in times past blamed and envied in manner for the same faults. For although Christ taught "they should give unto Caesar that which was Caesar's," yet was He charged with sedition, in that He was accused to devise some conspiracy and covet the kingdom. And hereupon they cried out with open mouth against him in the place of judgment: "If thou let this man escape, thou art not Caesar's friend." And though the Apostles did likewise evermore and steadfastly teach, that magistrates ought to be obeyed, "that every soul ought to be subject to the higher powers, not only for fear of wrath and punishment, but even for conscience sake;" yet bare they the name to disquiet the people, and to stir up the multitude to rebel. After this sort did Haman specially bring the nation of the Jews into the hatred of the king Assuerus, because, said he, "they were a rebellious and stubborn people, and despised the ordinances and commandments of princes." Wicked

King Ahab said to Elie [Elijah] the prophet of God, "It is thou that troublest Israel." Amasias, the priest at Bethel, laid a conspiracy to the prophet Amos' charge before King Jeroboam, saying, "See, Amos hath made a conspiracy against thee in the midst of the house of Israel." To be brief, Tertullian saith, this was the general accusation of all Christians while he lived, that they were traitors, they were rebels, and the enemies of mankind. Wherefore, if now-a-days the truth be likewise evil spoken of, and being the same truth it was then, if it be now like despitefully used as it was in times past, though it be a grievous and unkind dealing, yet can it not seem unto us a new or an unwonted matter.

Forty years ago and upward, was it an easy thing for them to devise against us these accursed speeches, and other, too, sorer than these; when, in the midst of the darkness of that age, first began to spring and to give shine some one glimmering beam of truth, unknown at that time and unheard of: when also Martin Luther and Hulderic Zuinglius, being most excellent men, even sent of God to give light to the whole world, first came unto the knowledge and preaching of the Gospel; whereas yet the thing was but new, and the success thereof uncertain; and when men's minds stood doubtful and amazed, and their ears open to all slanderous tales; and when there could be imagined against us no fact so detestable, but the people then would soon believe it for the novelty and strangeness of the matter. For so did Symmachus, so did Celsus, so did Julianus, so did Porphyrius, the old foes to the Gospel, attempt in times past to accuse all Christians of sedition and treason, before that either prince or people were able to know who those Christians were, what they professed, what they believed, or what was their meaning. But now, sithence our very enemies do see, and cannot deny, but we ever in all our words and writings have diligently put the people in mind of their duty, to obey their princes and magistrates, yea, though they be wicked (for this doth very trial and experience sufficiently teach, and all men's eyes, whosoever and wheresoever they be, do well enough see and witness for us), it was a foul part of them to charge us with these things; yea, seeing they could find no new and late faults, therefore to seek to procure us envy only with stale and out worn lies.

We give our Lord God thanks, whose only cause this is, there hath yet at no time been any such example in all the realms, dominions, and commonweals, which have received the Gospel. For we have overthrown no kingdom, we have decayed no man's power or right, we have disordered no commonwealth. There continue in their own accustomed state and ancient dignity, the kings of our country of England, the kings of Denmark, the kings of Sweden, the dukes of Saxony, the counts palatine, the marquesses of Brandenburg, the landgraves of Hesse, the commonwealth of the Helvetians and Rhaetians, and the free cities, as Argentine, Basil, Frankfort, Ulm, Augusta, and Nuremberg; do all, I say, abide in the same authority and estate wherein they have been heretofore, or rather in a much better, for that by means of the Gospel they have their people more obedient unto them. Let them go, I pray you, into those places where at this present through God's goodness the Gospel is taught. Where is there more majesty? Where is there less arrogancy and tyranny? Where be the prince more honoured? Where is the people less unruly? Where hath there at any time the commonwealth or the Church been in more quiet? Perhaps ye will say, from the first beginning of this doctrine the common sort everywhere began to rage and to rise throughout Germany. Allow it were so, yet Martin Luther, the publisher and setter forward of this doctrine, did write marvellous vehemently and sharply against them, and reclaimed them, home to peace and obedience.

But whereas it is wont sometime to be objected by persons wanting skill touching the Helvetians' change of state, and killing of Leopoldus the Duke of Austria, and restoring by force their country to liberty, that was done, as appeareth plainly by all stories, for two hundred and threescore years past or above, under Boniface the Eighth, when the authority of the "Bishop of Rome" was in greatest jollity; about two hundred years before Huldericus Zuinglius either began to teach the Gospel, or yet was born: and ever since that time they have had all things still and quiet, not only from foreign enemies, but also from civil dissension. And if it were a sin in the Helvetians to deliver their own country from foreign government, specially when they were so proudly and tyrannously oppressed, yet to burden us with other men's faults, or them with the faults of their forefathers, is against all right and reason.

But O immortal God! and will the Bishop of Rome accuse us of treason? Will he teach the people to obey and follow their magistrates? or hath he any regard at all of the majesty of princes? Why doth he then, as none of the old bishops of Rome heretofore ever did, suffer himself to be called of his flatterers "lord of lords," as though he would have all kings and princes, who and whatsoever they are, to be his underlings? Why doth he vaunt himself to be "king of kings," and to have kingly royalty over his subjects? Why compelleth he all emperors and princes to swear to him fealty and true obedience? Why doth he boast that the "emperor's majesty's is a thousandfold inferior to him:" and for this reason specially, because God hath made two lights in heaven, and because heaven and earth were created not at two beginnings, but in one? Why hath he and his complices (like Anabaptists and Libertines, to the end they might run on more licentiously and carelessly) shaken off the yoke, and exempted themselves from being under a civil power? Why hath he his legates (as much to say as most subtle spies) lying in wait in all kings' courts, councils, and privy chambers? Why doth he, when he list, set Christian princes one against another, and at his own pleasure trouble the whole world with debate and discord? Why doth he excommunicate, and command to be taken as a heathen and a Pagan any Christian prince that renounceth his authority? And why promiseth he his "indulgences and his pardons" so largely to any that will (what way soever it be) kill any of his enemies? Doth he maintain empires and kingdoms? or doth he once desire that common quiet should be provided for? You must pardon us, good reader, though we seem to utter these things more bitterly and bitingly than it becometh divines to do. For both the shamefulness of the matter, and the desire of rule in the Bishop of Rome is so exceeding and outrageous, that it could not well be uttered with other words, or more mildly. For he is not ashamed to say in open assembly, "that all jurisdiction of all kings doth depend upon himself." And to feed his ambition and greediness of rule, he hath pulled in pieces the "empire of Rome," and vexed and rent whole Christendom asunder. Falsely and traitorously also did he release the Romans, the Italians, and himself too, of the oath whereby they and he were straitly bound to be true to the "emperor of Greece," and stirred up the emperor's subjects to forsake him: and calling Carolus Martellus out of France into Italy, made him emperor, such a thing as never was seen before. He put Chilpericus, the French king, being no evil prince, beside his realm, only because he fancied him not, and wrongfully placed Pipin in his room. Again, after he had cast out King Philip, if he could have brought it to pass, he had determined and appointed the kingdom of France to Albertus King of Romans. He utterly destroyed the state of the most nourishing city and commonweal of Florence, his own native country, and brought it out of a free and peaceable state, to be governed at the pleasure of one man: he brought to pass by his procurement, that whole Savoy on the one side was miserably spoiled by the Emperor Charles the Fifth, and on the other side by the French king, so as the unfortunate duke had scant one city left him to hide his head in.

We are cloyed with examples in this behalf, and it should be very tedious to reckon up all the notorious deeds of the bishops of Rome. Of which side were they, I beseech you, which poisoned Henry the Emperor even in the receiving of the sacrament? which poisoned Victor the Pope even in the receiving of the chalice? which poisoned our King John, king of England, in a drinking cup? Whosoever at least they were and of what sect soever, I am sure they were neither Lutherans nor Zuinglians. What is he at this day, which alloweth the mightiest kings and monarchs of the world to kiss his blessed feet? What is he that commandeth the emperor to go by him at his horse bridle, and the French king to hold his stirrup? Who hurled under his table Francis Dandalus the duke of Venice, king of Crete and Cyprus, fast bound with chains, to feed of bones among his dogs? Who set the imperial crown upon the Emperor Henry the Sixth's head, not with his hand, but with his foot; and with the same foot again cast the same crown off, saying withal, "he had power to make emperors, and to unmake them again at his pleasure"? Who put in arms Henry the son against the emperor his father Henry the Fourth, and wrought so that the father was taken prisoner of his own son, and being shorn and shamefully handled, was thrust into a monastery, where with hunger and sorrow he pined away to death? Who so ill-favouredly and monstrously put the Emperor Frederick's neck under his feet, and, as though that were not sufficient, added further this text out of the Psalms, "Thou shalt go upon the adder and cockatrice, and shalt tread the lion and dragon under thy feet"? Such an example of scorning and contemning a prince's majesty, as never before that was heard tell of in any remembrance; except, I ween, either of Tamerlane's, the king of Scythia, a wild and barbarous creature, or else of Sapor king of the Persians.

All these notwithstanding were Popes, all Peter's successors, all most holy fathers, whose several words we must take to be as good as several Gospels. If we be counted traitors which do honour our princes, which give them all obedience, as much as is due to them by God's word, and which do pray for them, what kind of men then be these, which have not only done all the things before said, but also allow the same for specially well done? Do they then either this way instruct the people, as we do, to reverence their magistrate? Or can they with honesty appeach us as seditious persons, breakers of the common quiet, and despisers of princes' majesty?

Truly, we neither put off the yoke of obedience from us; neither do we disorder realms; neither do we set up or pull down kings; nor translate governments; nor give our kings poison to drink; nor yet hold to them our feet to be kissed; nor, opprobriously triumphing over them, leap into their necks with our feet. This rather is our profession; this is our doctrine: that every soul, of what calling soever he be--be he monk, be he preacher, be he prophet, be he Apostle--ought to be subject to kings and magistrates; yea, and that the Bishop of Rome himself--unless he will seem greater than Evangelists, than the Prophets, or the Apostles--ought both to acknowledge and to call the emperor his lord and master, which the old Bishops of Rome, who lived in times of more grace, ever did. Our common teaching also is, that we ought so to obey princes as men sent of God; and that whoso withstandeth them, withstandeth God's ordinance. This is our showing, and this is well to be seen, both in our books and in our preachings, and also in the manners and modest behaviour of our people.

But where they say we have gone away from the unity of the Catholic Church, this is not only a matter of malice, but, besides, though, it be most untrue, yet hath it some show and appearance of truth. For the common people and ignorant multitude give not credit alone to things true and of certainty, but even to such things also, if any chance, which may seem to have but a resemblance of truth. Therefore, we see that subtle and crafty persons, when they had no truth on their side, have ever contended and hotly argued with things likely to be true, to the intent they which were not able to espy the very ground of the matter, might be carried away at least with some pretence and probability thereof. In times past, where the first Christians, our forefathers, in making their prayers to God, did turn themselves towards the east, there were that said, "they worshipped the sun, and reckoned it as God." Again, where our forefathers said, that as touching immortal and everlasting life, they lived by no other means, but by the "flesh and blood of that Lamb who was without spot," that is to say, of our Saviour Jesus Christ, the envious creatures and foes of Christ's Cross, whose only care was to bring Christian religion into slander by all manner of ways, made people believe that they were wicked persons, that they "sacrificed men's flesh, and drunk men's blood." Also, where our forefathers said that before God "there is neither man nor woman," nor, for attaining to the true righteousness, there is no distinction at all of persons, and that they did call one another indifferently by the name of sisters and brothers: there wanted not men which forged false tales upon the same, saying that the Christians made no difference among themselves either of age or of kind, but like brute beasts without regard had to do one with another. And where, for to pray and hear the Gospel, they met often together in secret and bye places, because rebels sometime were wont to do the like, rumours were everywhere spread abroad, how they made privy confederacies, and counselled together either to kill the magistrates or to subvert the commonwealth. And where, in celebrating the holy mysteries after Christ's institution, they took bread and wine, they were thought of many not to worship Christ, but Bacchus and Ceres; forsomuch as those vain gods were worshipped of the heathens in like sort, after a profane superstition, with bread and wine.

These things were believed of many, not because they were true, indeed (for what could be more untrue?), but because they were like to be true, and through a certain shadow of truth might the more easily deceive the simple. On this fashion likewise do these men slander us as heretics, and say that we have left the Church and fellowship of Christ: not because they think it is true--for they do not much force of that, but because to ignorant folk it might, perhaps, some way appear true. We have, indeed, put ourselves apart not as heretics are wont, from the Church of Christ, but as all good men ought to do, from the infection of naughty persons and hypocrites.

Nevertheless, in this point they triumph marvellously--"that they be the Church, that their Church is Christ's spouse, the pillar of truth, the ark of Noah;" and that without it there is no hope of salvation. Contrariwise they say, "that we be renegades; that we have torn Christ's seat;" that we are plucked quite off from the body of Christ, and have forsaken the Catholic faith. And when they leave nothing unspoken that may never so falsely and maliciously be said against us, yet this one thing are they never able truly to say, that we have swerved either from the Word of God, or from the Apostles of Christ, or from the primitive Church. Surely we have ever judged the primitive Church of Christ's time, of the Apostles and of the holy fathers, to be the Catholic Church; neither make we doubt to name it, "Noah's ark, Christ's spouse, the pillar and upholder of all truth;" nor yet to fix therein the whole mean of our salvation. It is doubtless an odious matter for one to leave the fellowship whereunto he hath been accustomed, and specially of those men, who, though they be not, yet at least seem and be called Christians. And, to say truly, we do not despise the Church of these men (howsoever it be ordered by them now-a-days), partly for the name's sake itself, and partly for that the Gospel of Jesus Christ hath once been therein truly and purely set forth. Neither had we departed therefrom, but of very necessity, and much against our wills. But I put case, an idol be set up in the Church of God, and the same desolation, which Christ prophesied to come, stood openly in the holy place. What if some thief or pirate invade and possess "Noah's ark?" These folks, as often as they tell us of the Church, mean thereby themselves alone, and attribute all these titles to their own selves, boasting, as they did in times past which cried, "The temple of the Lord, the temple of the Lord;" or as the Pharisees and Scribes did, which craked they were "Abraham's children."

Thus with a gay and jolly show deceive they the simple, and seek to choke us with the very name of the Church. Much like as if a thief, when he had gotten into another man's house, and by violence either hath thrust out or slain the owner, should afterward assign the same house to himself, casting forth of possession the right inheritor; or if Anti-Christ, when he had once entered into "the temple of God," should afterward say, "This house is mine own, and Christ hath nothing to do withal." For these men now, after they have left nothing remaining in the Church of God that hath any likeness of this Church, yet will they seem the patrons and valiant maintainers of the Church, very like as Gracchus amongst the Romans stood in defence of the treasury, notwithstanding with his prodigality and fond expenses he had utterly wasted the whole stock of the treasury. And yet was there never anything so wicked, or so far out of reason, but lightly it might be covered and defended by the name of the Church. For the wasps also make honey-combs as well as bees, and wicked men have companies like to the Church of God: yet, for all that, "they be not straightway the people of God which are called the people of God; neither be they all Israelites as many as are come of Israel the father." The Arians, notwithstanding they were heretics, yet bragged they that they alone were Catholics, calling all the rest now Ambrosians, now Athanasians, now Johannites. And Nestorius, as saith Theodoret, for all that he was an heretic, yet covered he himself [Greek text]: that is, to wit, with a certain cloak and colour of the true and right faith. Ebion, though he agreed in opinion with the Samaritans, yet, as saith Epiphanius, he would needs be called a Christian. The Mahometists at this day, for all that all histories make plain mention, and themselves also cannot deny, but they took their first beginning of "Agar the bond-woman," yet for the very name and stock's sake, chose they rather to be called Saracens, as though they came of "Sarah the free woman, and Abraham's wife."

So likewise the false prophets of all ages, which stood up against the prophets of God, which resisted Esaias, Jeremy, Christ, and the Apostles, at no time craked of anything so much as they did of the name of the Church. And for no other cause did they so fiercely vex them, and call them runaways and apostates, than for that they forsook their fellowship, and kept not the ordinances of the elders. Wherefore, if we would follow the judgments of those men only who then governed the Church, and would respect nothing else, neither God nor His word, it must needs be confessed, that the Apostles were rightly and by just law condemned of them to death, because they fell from the bishops and priests, that is, you must think, from the "Catholic Church:" and because they made many new alterations in religion, contrary to the bishops' and priests' wills, yea, and for all their spurning so earnestly against it. Wherefore, like as it is written that Hercules in old time was forced in striving with Antaeus, that huge giant, to lift him quite up from the earth that was his mother, ere he could conquer him, even so must our adversaries be heaved from their mother, that is, from this vain colour and shadow of the Church, wherewith they so disguise and defend themselves: otherwise they cannot be brought to yield unto the word of God. "And therefore," saith Jeremy the prophet, "make not such great boast that the temple of the Lord is with you. This is but a vain confidence: these are lies." The angel also saith in the Apocalypse, "They say they be Jews; but they be the synagogue of Satan." And Christ said to the Pharisees when they vaunted themselves of the kindred and blood of Abraham, "Ye are of your father, the devil;" for you resemble not your father Abraham; as much to say as ye are not the men ye would so fain be called: ye beguile the people with vain titles, and abuse the name of the Church to the overthrowing of the Church.

So that these men's part had been, first to have clearly and truly proved that the Romish Church is the true and right instructed Church of God, and that the same as they do order it at this day doth agree with the primitive Church of Christ, of the Apostles, and of the holy fathers, which we doubt not but was indeed the true Catholic Church. For our parts, if we could have judged ignorance, error, superstition, idolatry, men's inventions, and the same commonly disagreeing with the Holy Scriptures, either to please God or to be sufficient for the obtaining everlasting salvation; or if we could ascertain ourselves, that the word of God was written but for a time only, and afterward again ought to be abrogated and put away: or else that the sayings and commandments of God ought to be subject to man's will, that whatsoever

God saith and commandeth, except the Bishop of Rome willeth and commandeth the same, it must be taken as void and unspoken: if we could have brought ourselves to believe these things, we grant there had been no cause at all why we should have left these men's company. As touching that we have now done to depart from that Church, whose errors were proved and made manifest to the world, which Church also had already evidently departed from God's word: and yet not to depart so much from itself, as from the errors thereof; and not to do this disorderly or wickedly, but quietly and soberly; we have done nothing herein against the doctrine either of Christ or of His Apostles. For neither is the Church of God such as it may not be dusked with some spot, or asketh not sometime reparation. Else what needeth there so many assemblies and councils, without the which, as saith AEgidius, the Christian faith is not able to stand? "For look," saith he: "how often councils are discontinued, so often is the Church destitute of Christ." Or if there be no peril that harm may come to the Church, what need is there to retain to no purpose the names of bishops, as is now commonly used among them? For if there be no sheep that may stray, why be they called shepherds? If there be no city that may be betrayed, why be they called watchmen? If there be nothing that may run to ruin, why be they called pillars? Anon after the first creation of the world the Church of God began to spread abroad, and the same was instructed with the heavenly word which God Himself pronounced with His own mouth. It was also furnished with Divine ceremonies. It was taught by the Spirit of God, by the patriarchs and prophets, and continued so even till the time that Christ showed Himself to us in the flesh.

This notwithstanding, how often, O good God, in the meanwhile, and how horribly was the same Church darkened and decayed! Where was that Church then, when "all flesh upon earth had denied their own way?" Where was it, when amongst the number of the whole world there were only eight persons (and they neither all chaste and good) whom God's will was should be saved alive from that universal destruction and mortality? when Elie the prophet so lamentably and bitterly made moan, that "only himself was left" of all the whole world which did truly and duly worship God? and when Esay said, "The silver of God's people (that is, of the Church) was become dross: and that the same city, which aforetime had been faithful, was now become a harlot: and that in the same there was no part sound throughout the whole body, from the head to the foot?" or else, when Christ Himself said, "that the house of God was made by the Pharisees and priests a den of thieves?" Of a truth, the Church, even as a corn-field, except it be eared, manured, tilled, and trimmed, instead of wheat it will bring forth thistles, darnel, and nettles. For this cause did God send ever among both Prophets and Apostles, and last of all His "own Son," who might bring home the people into the right way, and repair anew the tottering Church after she had erred.

But lest some man should say, that the aforesaid things happened in the time of the law only, of shadows, and of infancy, when truth lay hid under figures and ceremonies, when nothing as yet was brought to perfection, when the law was not graven in men's hearts, but in stone: and yet is that but a foolish saying, for even at those days was there the very same God that is now, the same Spirit, the same Christ, the same faith, the same doctrine, the same hope, the same inheritance, the same league, and the same efficacy and virtue of God's word: Eusebius also saith: "All the faithful, even from Adam until Christ, were in very deed Christians" (though they were not so termed), but, as I said, lest men should thus speak still, Paul the Apostle found the like faults and falls even then in the prime and chief of the Gospel in chief perfection, and in the light; so that he was compelled to write in this sort to the Galatians, whom he had well before that instructed: "I fear me," quoth he, "lest I have laboured among you in vain, and lest ye have heard the Gospel in vain." "O my little children, of whom I travail anew till Christ be fashioned again in you." And as for the Church of the Corinthians, how foully it was denied, is nothing needful to rehearse. Now tell me, might the Churches of the Galatians and Corinthians go amiss, and the Church of Rome alone may not fail, nor go amiss? Surely Christ prophesied long before of His Church, that the time should come when desolation should stand in the holy place. And Paul saith, that Antichrist should once set up his own tabernacle and stately seat in the temple of God: and that the time should be, "when men should not away with wholesome doctrine, but be turned back unto fables and lies," and that within the very Church. Peter likewise telleth, how there should be teachers of lies in the Church of Christ. Daniel the Prophet, speaking of the latter times of Antichrist: "Truth," saith he, "in that season shall be thrown under foot, and trodden upon in the world." And Christ saith, how the calamity and confusion of things shall be so exceeding great, "that even the chosen, if it were possible, shall be brought into error;" and how all these things shall come to pass, not amongst Gentiles and Turks, but that they should be in the holy place, in the temple of

God, in the Church, and in the company and fellowship of those which profess the name of Christ.

Albeit these same warnings alone may suffice a wise man to take heed he do not suffer himself rashly to be deceived with the name of the Church, and not to stay to make further inquisition thereof by God's word; yet beside all this, many fathers also, many learned and godly men, have often and carefully complained how all these things have chanced in their lifetime. For even in the midst of that thick mist of darkness, God would yet there should be some, who, though they gave not a clear and bright light, yet should they kindle, were it but some spark, which men might espy, being in the darkness.

Hilarius, when things as yet were almost uncorrupt, and in good ease too: "Ye are ill deceived," saith he, "with the love of walls: ye do ill worship the Church, in that ye worship it in houses and buildings: ye do ill bring in the name of peace under roofs. Is there any doubt but Antichrist will have his seat under the same? I rather reckon hills, woods, pools, marshes, prisons, and quagmires, to be places of more safety: for in these the prophets, either abiding of their accord or forced thither by violence, did prophesy by the Spirit of God."

Gregory, as one which perceived and foresaw in his mind the wrack of all things, wrote thus to "John, Bishop of Constantinople," the first of all others that commanded himself to be called by this new name, the "universal bishop of whole Christ's Church:" "If the Church," saith he, "shall depend upon one man, it will at once fall down to the ground." Who is he, that seeth not how this is come to pass long since? For long agone hath the Bishop of Rome willed to have the "whole Church depend upon" himself alone. Wherefore it is no marvel though it be clean fallen down long agone.

Bernard the abbot, above four hundred years past, writeth thus: "Nothing is now of sincerity and pureness amongst the clergy: wherefore it resteth, that the man of sin should be revealed." The same Bernard, in his work of the conversion of Paul; "It seemeth now," saith he, "that persecution hath ceased: no, no; persecution seemeth but now to begin, even from them which have chief pre-eminence in the Church. Thy friends and neighbours have drawn near, and stood up against thee: from the sole of thy foot to the crown of thy head there is no part whole. Iniquity is proceeded from the elders, the judges, and deputies, which pretend to rule thy people. We cannot say now, Look how the people be, so is the priest. For the people is not so ill as the priest is. Alas, alas, O Lord God, the selfsame persons be the chief in persecuting thee, which seem to love the highest place, and bear most rule in Thy Church!" The same Bernard again, upon the Canticles, writeth thus: "All they are thy friends, yet are they all thy foes: all thy kinsfolk, yet are they all thy adversaries. Being Christ's servants, they serve Antichrist. Behold, in my rest, my bitterness is most bitter." Roger Bacon, also a man of great fame, after he had in a vehement oration touched to the quick the woeful state of his own time: "These so many errors," saith he, "require and look for Antichrist." Gerson complaineth, that in his days all the substance and efficacy of sacred divinity was brought unto a glorious contention and ostentation of wits, and to very sophistry. The friars of Lyons, men, as touching the manner of their life, not to be misliked, were wont boldly to affirm, that the Romish Church (from whence alone all counsel and order was then sought) was the very same "harlot of Babylon and rout of devils," whereof is prophesied so plainly in the Apocalypse.

I know well enough the authority of these foresaid persons is but lightly regarded among these men. How then if I call forth those for witness, whom they themselves have used to honour? What if I say that Adrian, the Bishop of Rome, did frankly confess that all these mischiefs brast out first from the high throne of the Pope? Pighius acknowledgeth herein to be a fault, that many abuses are brought in, even into the very mass, which mass otherwise he would have seem to be a reverend matter. Gerson saith, that through the number of most fond ceremonies, all the virtue of the Holy Ghost, which ought to have operation in us, and all true godliness, is utterly quenched and dead. Whole Greece and Asia complain, how the bishops of Rome, with the marts of their purgatories and pardons, have both tormented men's consciences and picked their purses.

As touching the tyranny of the bishops of Rome, and their barbarous Persian-like pride, to leave out others, whom perchance they reckon for enemies, because they freely and liberally find fault with their vices, the same men which have led their life at Rome in the holy city, in the face of the most holy father, who also were able to see all their secrets and at no time departed from the Catholic faith: as, for example, Laurentius Valla, Marsilius Patavinus, Francis Petrarch, Hierom Savonarola, Abbot Joachim, Baptist of Mantua, and, before all these, Bernard the abbot, have many a time and much complained of it, giving the world also sometime to understand that the Bishop of Rome himself (by your leave) is very Antichrist. Whether they spake it truly or falsely, let that go. Sure I am they spake it plainly. Neither can any man allege that those authors were Luther's or Zuinglius' scholars: for they were not only certain years, but also certain ages ere ever Luther's or Zuinglius' names were heard of. They well saw that even in their days errors had crept into the Church, and wished earnestly they might be amended.

And what marvel if the Church were then carried away with errors in that time, specially when neither the Bishop of Rome, who then only ruled the roost, nor almost any other, either did his duty, or once understood what was his duty? for it is hard to be believed, while they were idle and fast asleep, that the devil also all that while either fell asleep or else continually lay idle. For how they were occupied in the meantime, and with what faithfulness they took care of God's house, though we hold our peace, yet I pray you, let them hear Bernard their own friend. "The bishops," saith he, "who now have the charge of God's Church, are not teachers, but deceivers: they are not feeders, but beguilers: they are not prelates, but Pilates." These words spake Bernard of that bishop who named himself the highest bishop of all, and of the other bishops likewise which then had the place of government. Bernard was no Lutheran: Bernard was no heretic. He had not forsaken the Catholic Church: yet nevertheless he did not let to call the bishops that then were, deceivers, beguilers, and Pilates. Now when the people was openly deceived, and Christian men's eyes were craftily bleared, and when Pilate sat in judgment-place, and condemned Christ and Christ's members to sword and fire, O good Lord, in what case was Christ's Church then? But yet tell me, of so many and so gross errors, what one have these men at any time reformed? or what fault have they once acknowledged and confessed?

But, forsomuch as these men avouch the universal possession of the Catholic Church to be their own, and call us heretics, because we agree not in judgment with them, let us know, I beseech you, what proper mark and badge hath that Church of theirs, whereby it may be known to be the Church of God. I wiss it is not so hard a matter to find out God's Church, if a man will seek it earnestly and diligently. For the Church of God is set upon a high and glittering place, in the top of a hill, and built upon the "foundation of the Apostles and Prophets:" "There," saith Augustine, "let us seek the Church; there let us try our matters." "And," as he saith again in another place, "the Church must be showed out of the holy and canonical Scriptures: and that which cannot be showed out of them is not the Church." Yet, for all this, I wot not how, whether it be for fear, or for conscience, or despair of victory, these men alway abhor and fly the Word of God, even as the thief flieth the gallows. And no wonder truly. For, like as men say, the cantharus by-and-bye perisheth and dieth as soon as it is laid in balm: notwithstanding balm be otherwise a most sweet-smelling ointment; even so these men well see their own matter is damned and destroyed in the Word of God, as if it were in poison.

Therefore the Holy Scriptures, which our Saviour Jesus Christ did not only use for authority in all His speech, but did also at last seal up the same with His own blood, these men, to the intent they might with less business drive the people from the same, as from a thing dangerous and deadly, have used to call them a bare letter, uncertain, unprofitable, dumb, killing, and dead: which seemeth to us all one as if they should say, "The Scriptures are to no purpose, or as good as none." Hereunto they add a similitude not very agreeable, how the Scriptures be like to a nose of wax, or a shipman's hose: how they may be fashioned and plied all manner of ways, and serve all men's turns. Woteth not the Bishop of Rome, that these things are spoken by his own minions? or understandeth he not he hath such champions to fight for him? Let him hearken then how holily and how godly one Hosius writeth of this matter, a bishop in Polonia, as he testifieth of himself; a man doubtless well spoken and not unlearned, and a very sharp and stout maintainer of that side. One will marvel, I suppose, how a good man could either conceive so wickedly or write so despitefully of those words which he knew proceeded from God's mouth, and specially in such sort as he would not have it seem his own private opinion alone, but the common opinion of all that band. He dissembleth, I grant you indeed, and hideth what he is, and setteth forth the matter so, as though it were not he and his side, but the Zuenckfeldian heretics that so did speak. "We," saith he, "will bid away with the same Scriptures, whereof we see brought not only divers but also contrary interpretations; and we will hear God speak, rather than we will resort to the naked elements, and appoint our salvation to rest in them. It behoveth not a man to be expert in the law and Scripture, but to be taught of God. It is but lost labour that a man bestoweth in the Scriptures. For the Scripture is a creature, and a certain bare letter." This is Hosius' saying, uttered altogether with the same spirit and the same mind wherewith in times past Montane and Marcion were moved, who, as men report, used to say, when with a contempt they rejected the Holy Scriptures, that themselves knew many more and better things than either Christ or the Apostles ever knew.

What then shall I say here, O ye principal posts of religion, O ye arch- governors of Christ's Church! Is this that your reverence which ye give to God's Word? The Holy Scriptures, which, St. Paul saith, came by the inspiration of God, which God did commend by so many miracles, wherein are the most perfect prints of Christ's own steps, which all the holy fathers, Apostles, and Angels, which Christ Himself the Son of God, as often as was needful, did allege for testimony and proof; will ye, as though they were unworthy for you to hear, bid them avaunt away? That is, will ye enjoin God to keep silence, who speaketh to you most clearly by His own mouth in the Scriptures? or that Word, whereby alone, as Paul saith, we are reconciled to God, and which the prophet David saith, is "holy and pure, and shall last for ever;" will ye call that "but a bare and dead letter?" or will ye say that all our labour is lost which is bestowed in that thing which Christ hath commanded us diligently to search, and to have evermore before our eyes? And will ye say that Christ and the Apostles meant with subtlety to deceive the people when they exhorted them to read the Holy Scriptures, that thereby they might flow in all wisdom and knowledge? No marvel at all though these men despise us and all our doings, which set so little by God Himself and His infallible sayings. Yet was it but want of wit in them, to the intend they might hurt us, to do so extreme injury to the Word of God.

But Hosius will here make exclamation, saying we do him wrong, and that these be not his own words, but the words of the heretic Zuenckfeldius. But how then, if Zuenckfeldius make exclamation on the other side, and say, that the same very words be not his, but Hosius' own words? For tell me where hath Zuenckfeldius ever written them? or, if he have written them, and

Hosius have judged the same to be wicked, why hath not Hosius spoken so much as one word to confute them? Howsoever the matter goeth, although Hosius peradventure will not allow of those words, yet he doth not disallow the meaning of the words For well near in all controversies, and namely touching the use of the holy "communion under both kinds," although the words of Christ be plain and evident, yet doth Hosius disdainfully reject them, as no better than "cold and dead elements;" and commandeth us to give faith to certain new lessons, appointed by the Church, and to I wot not what revelations of the Holy Ghost. And Pighius saith: "Men ought not to believe, no not the most clear and manifest words of the Scriptures, unless the same be allowed for good by the interpretation and authority of the Church."

And yet, as though this were too little, they also burn the Holy Scriptures, as in times past wicked King Aza did, or as Antiochus or Maximinus did, and are wont to name them heretics' books. And out of doubt, to see too, they would fain do as Herod in old time did in Jewry, that he might with more surety keep still his dominion: who being an Idumaean born, and a stranger to the stock and kindred of the Jews, and yet coveting much to be taken for a Jew, to the end he might establish to him and his posterity the kingdom of that country, which he had gotten of Augustus Caesar, he commanded all the genealogies and pedigrees to be burnt, and made out of the way, so that there should remain no record whereby he might be known to them that came after that he was an alien in blood: whereas even from Abraham's time these monuments had been safely kept amongst the Jews, and laid up in their treasury; because in them it might easily and most assuredly be found of what lineage everyone did descend.

So (in good faith) do these men, when they would have all their own doings in estimation, as though they had been delivered to us even from the Apostles, or from Christ Himself: to the end there might be found nowhere anything able to convince such their dreams and lies, either they burn the Holy Scriptures, or else they craftily convey them from the people surely.

Very rightly and aptly doth Chrysostom write against these men. "Heretics," saith he, "shut up the doors against the truth: for they know full well, if the door were open, the Church should be none of theirs." Theophylact also: "God's Word," saith he, "is the candle whereby the thief is espied." And Tertullian saith, "The Holy Scripture manifestly findeth out the fraud and theft of heretics." For why do they hide, why do they keep under the Gospel which Christ would have preached aloud from the house-top? Why whelm they that light under a bushel which ought to stand on a candlestick? Why trust they more to the blindness of the unskilful multitude, and to ignorance, than to the goodness of their cause? Think they their sleights are not already perceived, and that they can walk now unespied, as though they had Gyges' ring, to go invisibly by, upon their finger? No, no. All men see now well and well again, what good stuff is in that chest of the "Bishop of Rome's bosom." This thing alone of itself may be an argument sufficient that they work not uprightly and truly. Worthily ought that matter seem suspicious which flieth trial, and is afraid of the light. "For he that doeth evil," as Christ saith, "seeketh darkness, and hateth the light." A conscience that knoweth itself clear cometh willingly into open show, that the works which proceed of God may be seen. Neither be they so very blind but they see this well enough, that their own kingdom straightway is at a point if the Scriptures once have the upper hand: and that, like as men say, the idols of devils in times past, of whom men in doubtful matters were then wont to receive answers, were suddenly stricken dumb at the sight of Christ, when He was born and came into the world: even so they see that now all their subtle practices will soon fall down headlong upon the sight of the Gospel. For Antichrist is not overthrown but by the brightness of Christ's coming.

As for us, we run not for succour to the fire, as these men's guise is, but we run to the Scriptures; neither do we reason with the sword, but with the Word of God: and therewith, as saith Tertullian "do we feed our faith; by it do we stir up our hope, and strengthen our confidence." For we know that the "Gospel of Jesus Christ is the power of God unto salvation;" and that therein consisteth eternal life. And as Paul warneth us, "We do not hear, no, not an Angel of God coming from Heaven, if he go about to pull us from any part of this doctrine." Yea, more than this, as the holy martyr Justin speaketh of himself, we would give no credence to God Himself, if He should teach us any other Gospel.

For where these men bid the Holy Scriptures away, as dumb and fruitless, and procure us to come to God Himself rather, who speaketh in the Church and in councils, which is to say, to believe their fancies and opinions; this way of finding out the truth is very uncertain and exceeding dangerous, and in manner a fantastical and mad way, and by no means allowed of the holy fathers. Chrysostom saith, "There be many oftentimes which boast themselves of the Holy Ghost; but truly whoso speak of their own head do falsely boast they have the Spirit of God. For like as (saith he) Christ denied He spake of Himself, when He spake out of the law and Prophets, even so now, if anything be pressed upon us in the Name of the Holy Ghost, save the Gospel, we ought not to believe it. For as Christ is the fulfilling of the law and Prophets, so is the Holy Ghost the fulfilling of the Gospel." Thus far goeth Chrysostom.

PART V

But here I look they will say, though they have not the Scriptures, yet may chance they have the ancient doctors and the holy fathers with them. For this is a high brag they have ever made, how that all antiquity and a continual consent of all ages doth make on their side; and that all our cases be but new, and yesterday's work, and until these few late years were never heard of. Questionless, there can nothing be more spitefully spoken against the religion of God than to accuse it of novelty, as a new come up matter. For as there can be no change in God Himself, so ought there to be no change in His religion.

Yet, nevertheless, we wot not by what means, but we have ever seen it come so to pass from the first beginning of all, that as often as God did give but some light, and did open His truth unto men, though the truth were not only of greatest antiquity, but also from everlasting; yet of wicked men and of the adversaries was it called new-fangled and of late devised. That ungracious and bloodthirsty Haman, when he sought to procure the king Assuerus' displeasure against the Jews, this was his accusation to him: "Thou hast here (saith he) a kind of people that useth certain new laws of their own, but stiff-necked and rebellious against all thy laws." When Paul also began first to preach and expound the Gospel at Athens he was called a tidings-bringer of new gods, as much to say as of a new religion; "for" (said the Athenians) "may we not know of thee what new doctrine this is?" Celsus likewise, when he of set purpose wrote against Christ, to the end he might more scornfully scoff out the Gospel by the name of novelty: "What!" saith he, "hath God after so many ages now at last and so late bethought Himself?" Eusebius also writeth that Christian religion from the beginning for very spite was called [Greek text], that is to say, new and strange. After like sort, these men condemn all our matters as strange and new; but they will have their own, whatsoever they are, to be praised as things of long continuance. Doing much like to the enchanters and sorcerers now-a-days, which working with devils, use to say they have their books and all their holy and hid mysteries from Athanasius, Cyprian, Moses, Abel, Adam, and from the archangel Raphael; because that their cunning, coming from such patrons and founders, might be judged the more high and holy. After the same fashion these men, because they would have their own religion, which they themselves, and that not long since, have brought forth into the world, to be the more easily and rather accepted of foolish persons, or of such as cast little whereabouts they or other do go, they are wont to say they had it from Augustine, Hierom, Chrysostom, from the Apostles, and from Christ Himself.

Full well know they that nothing is more in the people's favour, or better liketh the common sort, than these names. But how if the things, which these men are so desirous to have seem new, be found of greatest antiquity? Contrariwise, how if all the things well-nigh which they so greatly set out with the name of antiquity, having been well and thoroughly examined, be at length found to be but new, and devised of very late? Soothly to say, no man that hath a true and right consideration would think the Jews' laws and ceremonies to be new, for all Haman's accusation. For they were graven in very ancient tables of most antiquity. And although many did take Christ to have swerved from Abraham and the old fathers, and to have brought in a certain new religion in His own Name, yet answered He them directly, "If ye believed Moses, ye would believe Me also," for My doctrine is not so new as you make it: for Moses, an author of greatest antiquity, and one to whom ye give all honour, "hath spoken of Me." Paul likewise, though the Gospel of Jesus Christ be of many counted to be but new, yet hath it (saith he) the testimony most old both of the law and Prophets. As for our doctrine which we may rightly call Christ's catholic doctrine, it is so far off from new that God, who is above all most ancient, and the Father of our Lord Jesus Christ, hath left the same unto us in the Gospel, in the Prophets' and Apostles' works, being monuments of greatest age. So that no man can now think our doctrine to be new, unless the same think either the Prophets' faith, or the Gospel, or else Christ Himself to be new.

And as for their religion, if it be of so long continuance as they would have men ween it is, why do they not prove it so by the examples of the primitive Church, and by the fathers and councils of old times? Why lieth so ancient a cause thus long in the dust destitute of an advocate? Fire and sword they have had always ready at hand, but as for the old councils and the fathers, all mum--not a word. They did surely against all reason to begin first with these so bloody and extreme means, if they could have found other more easy and gentle ways. And if they trust so fully to antiquity, and use no dissimulation, why did John Clement, a countryman of ours, but few years past, in the presence of certain honest men and of good credit, tear and cast into the fire certain leaves of Theodoret--the most ancient father and a Greek bishop--wherein he plainly and evidently taught that the nature of bread in the Communion was not changed, abolished, or brought to nothing? And this did he of purpose, because he thought there was no other copy thereof to be found. Why saith Albertus Pighius that the ancient father Augustine had a wrong opinion of original sin? and that he erred and lied and used false logic, as touching the case of matrimony concluded after a vow made, which Augustine affirmeth to be perfect matrimony, indeed, and cannot be undone again? Also when they did of late put in print the ancient father Origen's work upon the Gospel of John, why left they quite out the whole sixth chapter? Wherein it is likely, yea, rather, of very surety, that the said Origen had written many things concerning the sacrament of the Holy Communion contrary to these men's minds; and would put forth that book mangled rather than full and perfect, for fear it should reprove them and their partners of their error. Call ye this trusting to antiquity, when ye rent in pieces, keep back, maim, and burn the ancient fathers' works?

It is a world to see, how well-favouredly and how towardly touching religion these men agree with the fathers of whom they use to vaunt that they be their own good. The old Council Eliberine made a decree that nothing that is honoured of the people should be painted in the churches. The old father Epiphanius saith:--"It is a horrible wickedness, and a sin not to be suffered, for any man to set up any picture in the Church of the Christians, yea, though it were the picture of Christ Himself." Yet, these men store all their temples, and each corner of them, with painted and carved images, as though without them religion were nothing worth.

The old fathers Origen and Chrysostom exhort the people to read the Scriptures, to buy them books, to reason at home betwixt themselves of divine matters--wives with their husbands, and parents with their children. These men condemn the Scriptures as dead elements, and--as much as ever they may--bar the people from them. The ancient fathers, Cyprian, Epiphanius, and Hierom, say, for one who, perchance, hath made a vow to lead a sole life, and afterwards liveth unchastely, and cannot quench the flames of lust, "it is better to marry a wife, and to live honestly in wedlock." And the old father Augustine judgeth the selfsame marriage to be good and perfect, and that it ought not to be broken again. These men, if a man have once bound himself by a vow, though afterwards he burn, keep queans, and defile himself with never so sinful and desperate a life, yet they suffer not that person to marry a wife; or if he chance to marry, they allow it not for marriage. And they commonly teach it is much better and more godly to keep a concubine and harlot, than to live in that kind of marriage.

The old father Augustine complained of the multitude of ceremonies, wherewith he even then saw men's minds and consciences overcharged. These men, as though God regarded nothing else but their ceremonies, have so out of measure increased them, that there is now almost none other thing left in their churches and places of prayer.

Again, that old father Augustine denieth it to be lawful for a monk to spend his time slothfully and idly, and, under a pretended and counterfeit holiness, to live all upon others. And whoso thus liveth, the old father Apollonius likeneth him to a thief. These men have, I wot not whether to name them droves or herds of monks, who for all they do nothing, nor yet once intend to bear any show of holiness, yet live they not only upon others, but also riot lavishly of other folks' labours.

The old council of Rome decreed that no man should come to the service said by a priest well known to keep a concubine. These men let to farm concubines to their priests, and yet constrain men by force against their will to hear their cursed paltry service.

The old canons of the Apostles command that bishop to be removed from his office, which will both supply the place of a civil magistrate, and also of an ecclesiastical person. These men, for all that, both do and will needs serve both places. Nay, rather, the one office which they ought chiefly to execute, they once touch not, and yet nobody commandeth them to be displaced.

The old Council Gangrense commandeth that none should make such difference between an unmarried priest and a married priest, as he ought to think the one more holy than the other for single life's sake. These men put such a difference between them, that they straightway think all their holy service to be defiled if it be done by a good and honest man that hath a wife.

The ancient emperor Justinian commanded that, in the holy administration, all things should be pronounced with a clear, loud, and treatable voice, that the people might receive some fruit thereby. These men, lest the people should understand them, mumble up all their service, not only with a drowned and hollow voice, but also in a strange and barbarous tongue.

The old council at Carthage commanded that nothing should be read in Christ's congregation but the canonical Scriptures. These men read such things in their churches as themselves know of a truth to be stark lies and fond fables.

But if there be any that think these above-rehearsed authorities be but weak and slender, because they were decreed by emperors and certain petit bishops, and not by so full and perfect councils, taking pleasure rather in the authority and name of the Pope, let such a one know that Pope Julius doth evidently forbid that the priest, in ministering the Communion, should dip the bread in the cup. These men, contrary to Pope Julius' decree, divide the bread, and dip it in the wine.

Pope Clement saith it is not lawful for a bishop to deal with both swords: "For if thou wilt have both," said he, "thou shalt deceive both thyself and those that obey thee." Nowadays, the Pope challengeth to himself both swords, and useth both. Wherefore, it ought to seem less marvel if that have followed which Clement saith, that is, "that he hath deceived both his own self and those which have given ear unto him."

Pope Leo saith, "Upon one day it is lawful to say but one mass in one church." These men say daily in one church commonly ten masses, twenty, thirty, yea, oftentimes more. So that the poor gazer on can scant tell which way he were best to turn him.

Pope Gelasius saith, "It is a wicked deed and sibb to sacrilege in any man to divide the Communion, and when he hath received one kind to abstain from the other." These men, contrary to God's Word, and contrary to Pope Gelasius, command that one kind only of the Holy Communion be given to the people, and by so doing they make their priests guilty of sacrilege.

But if they will say that all these things are worn out of ure and nigh dead, and pertain nothing to these present times, yet to the end all folk may understand what faith is to be given to these men, and upon what hope they call together their general councils, let us see in few words what good heed they take to the selfsame thing, which they themselves these very last years (and the remembrance thereof is yet new and fresh), in their own general council that they had by order called, have decreed and commanded to be devoutly kept. In the last council at Trent, scant fourteen years past, it was ordained by the common consent of all degrees, "that one man should not have two benefices at one time." What is become now of that ordinance? Is the same too soon worn out of mind, and clean consumed? For these men, ye see, give to one man not two benefices only, but sundry abbeys many times, sometimes also two bishoprics, sometimes three, sometimes four. And that not only to an unlearned man, but oftentimes also even to a man of war.

In the said council a decree was made that all bishops should preach the Gospel. These men neither preach nor once go up into the pulpit, neither think they it any part of their office. What great pomp and crake then is this they make of antiquity? Why brag they so of the names of the ancient fathers, and of the new and old councils? Why will they seem to trust to their authority whom when they list they despise at their pleasure?

But I have a special fancy to commune a word or two rather with the Pope's good holiness, and to say these things to his own face. Tell us, I pray you, good holy father, seeing ye do crake so much of all antiquity, and boast yourself that all men are bound to you alone, which of all the fathers hath at any time called you by the name of the "highest prelate," the "universal bishop," or the "head of the Church"? Which of them ever said "that both the swords were committed unto you?" Which of them ever said "that you have authority and right to call councils?" Which of them ever said "the whole world is but your diocese?" Which of them "that all bishops have received of your fulness?" Which of them "that all power is given to you as well in heaven as in earth?" Which of them "that neither kings, nor the whole clergy, nor yet all the people together, are able to be judges over you?" Which of them "that kings and emperors, by Christ's commandment and will, do receive authority at your hands?" Which of them with so precise and mathematical limitation hath surveyed and determined you to be "seventy and seven times greater than the mightiest kings?" Which of them that more ample authority is given to you than to the residue of the patriarchs? Which of them that you are the "Lord God"? or that you are "not a mere natural man, but a certain substance made and grown together of God and man"? Which of them that you are the only "head-spring of all laws"? Which of them that you have "power over purgatories?" Which of them that you are able to "command the angels of God" as you list yourself? Which of them that ever said that you are "lord of lords" and the "king of kings"? We can also go further with you in like sort. What one amongst the whole number of the old bishops and fathers ever taught you either to say private mass while the people stared on, or to "lift up the Sacrament" over your head (in which point consisteth now all your religion), or else to "mangle Christ's Sacraments," and to bereave the people of the one part, contrary to Christ's institution and plain express words? But that we may once come to an end, what one is there of all the fathers which hath taught you to distribute Christ's blood and the holy martyrs' merits, and to sell openly as merchandises your pardons and all the rooms and lodgings of purgatory?

These men are wont to speak much of a certain secret doctrine of theirs, and of their manifold and sundry readings. Then let them bring forth somewhat now, if they can, that it may appear they have at least read or do know somewhat. They have often stoutly noised in all corners where they went how all the parts of their religion be very old, and have been approved not only of the multitude, but also by the consent and continual observation of all nations and times. Let them, therefore, once in their life show this their antiquity. Let them make appear at eye that the things whereof they make such ado have taken so long and large increase. Let them declare that all Christian nations have agreed by consent to this their religion.

Nay, nay, they turn their backs, as we have said already, and flee from their own decrees, and have cut off and abolished again within a short space the same things which, but a few years before, themselves had established for evermore, forsooth, to continue. How should one, then, trust them in the fathers, in the old councils, and in the words spoken by God? They have not, good Lord, they have not, I say, those things which they boast they have: they have not that antiquity, they have not that universality, they have not that consent of all places, nor of all times. And though they have a desire rather to dissemble, yet they themselves are not ignorant hereof: yea, and sometime also they let not to confess it openly. And for this cause they say that the ordinances of the old councils and fathers be such as may now and then be altered, and that sundry and divers decrees serve for sundry and divers times of the Church. Thus lurk they under the name of the Church, and beguile silly creatures with their vain glozing. It is to be marvelled that either men be so blind that they cannot see this, or if they see it, to be so patient as they can lightly and quietly bear it.

But, whereas they have commanded that those decrees should be void, as things now waxen too old, and that have lost their grace, perhaps they have provided in their stead certain other better things, and more profitable for the people. For it is a common saying with them that, "if Christ Himself or the Apostles were alive again, they could not better nor godlier govern God's Church than it is at this present governed by them." They have put in their stead indeed; but it is "chaff instead of wheat," as Hieremy saith, and such things as, according to Esay's words, "God never required at their hands." "They have stopped up," saith he, "all the veins of clear springing water, and have digged up for the people deceivable and puddle-like pits, full of mire and filth, which neither have nor are able to hold pure water." They have plucked away from the people the Holy Communion, the Word of God, from whence all comfort should be taken; the true worshipping of God also, and the right use of sacraments and prayer; and have given us of their own to play withal in the meanwhile, salt, water, oil, boxes, spittle, palms, bulls, jubilees, pardons, crosses, censings, and an endless rabble of ceremonies, and, as a man might term with Plautus, "pretty games to make sport withal." In these things have they set all their religion, teaching the people that by these God may be duly pacified, spirits be driven away, and men's consciences well quieted. For these, lo, be the orient colours and precious savours of Christian religion; these things doth God look upon and accepteth them thankfully; these must come in place to be honoured, and put quite away the institutions of Christ and of His Apostles. And like as in times past, when wicked King Jeroboam had taken from the people the right serving of God, and brought them to worship the golden calves, lest perchance they might afterward change their mind and slip away, getting them again to Jerusalem to the temple of God, there he exhorted them with a long tale to be steadfast, saying thus unto them: "O Israel, these calves be thy gods. In this sort commanded your God you should worship Him, for it should be wearisome and troublous for you to take upon you a journey so far off, and yearly to go up to Jerusalem, there to serve and honour your God." Even after the same sort every whit, when these men had once made the law of God of non- effect through their own traditions, fearing that the people should afterward open their eyes and fall another way, and should somewhence else seek a surer mean of their salvation, Jesu, how often have they cried out, "This is the same worshipping that pleaseth God, and which He straitly requireth of us, and wherewith He will be turned from His wrath. That by these things is conserved the unity of the Church. By these all sins be cleansed, and consciences quieted, and that whoso departeth from these hath left unto himself no hope of everlasting salvation." For it were wearisome and troublous, say they, for the people to resort to Christ, to the Apostles, and to the ancient fathers, and to observe continually what their will and commandment should be. This ye may see, is to "withdraw the people of God from the weak elements of the world, from the leaven of the Scribes and Pharisees, and from the traditions of men." It were reason, no doubt, that Christ's commandments and the Apostles' were removed, that these their devices might come in place. O just cause, I promise you, why that ancient and so long allowed doctrine should be now abolished, and a new form of religion be brought into the Church of God.

And yet whatever it be, these men cry still that nothing ought to be changed: that men's minds are well satisfied herewithal: that the Church of Rome, the Church which cannot err, hath decreed these things. For Silvester Prierias saith, that the Romish Church is the squire and rule of truth, and that the Holy Scripture hath received from thence authority and credit. "The doctrine," saith he, "of the Romish Church is the rule of most infallible faith, from the which the Holy Scripture taketh his force. And indulgences and pardons, saith he, are not made known to us by the authority of the Scriptures, but they are made known to us by the authority of the Romish Church, and of the Bishops of Rome, which is greater." Pighius also letteth not to say, that without the license of the Romish Church, we ought not to believe the very plain Scriptures. Much like as if any of those that cannot speak pure and clean Latin, and yet can babble out quickly and readily a little some such law Latin as serveth the court, would needs hold that all others ought also to speak after the same way which Mammetrectus and Catholicon spake many years ago, and which themselves do yet use in pleading in court: for so may it be understood sufficiently what is said, and men's desires be satisfied: and that it is a fondness now in the latter end to trouble the world with a new kind of speaking, and to call again the old finesse and eloquence that Cicero and Caesar used in their days in the Latin tongue. So much are these men beholden to the folly and darkness of the former times. "Many things," as one writeth, "are had in estimation oftentimes, because they have been once dedicate to the temples of the heathen gods." Even so we see at this day many things allowed and highly set by of these men, not because they judge them so much worth, but only because they have been received into a custom, and after a sort dedicate to the temple of God.

"Our Church," say they, "cannot err." They speak that, I think, as the Lacedaemonians long since used to say, that it was not possible to find any adulterer in all their commonwealth: whereas indeed they were rather all adulterers, and had no certainty in their marriages, but had their wives common amongst them all: or as the canonists at this day, for their bellies' sake, used to say of the Pope, that forsomuch as he is lord of all benefices, though he sell for money bishoprics, monasteries, priesthood, spiritual promotions, and part with nothing freely, yet, because he counteth all his own, "he cannot commit simony, though he would never so fain." But how strongly and agreeably to reason these things be spoken, we are not as yet able to perceive, except perchance these men have plucked off the wings from the truth; as the Romans in old time did prune and pinion their goddess Victoria, after they had once gotten her home, to the end that with the same wings she should never more be able to flee away from them again. But what if Jeremy tell them, as is afore rehearsed, that these be lies? What if the same prophet say in another place that the selfsame men, who ought to be keepers of the vineyard, have brought to nought and destroyed the Lord's vineyard? How if Christ say that the same persons, who chiefly ought to have care over the temple, have made of the Lord's temple a den of thieves? If it be so that the Church of Rome cannot err, it must needs follow, that the good luck thereof is far greater than all these men's policy. For such is their life, their doctrine, and their diligence, that for all them the Church may not only err, but also utterly be spoiled and perish. No doubt, if that church may err which hath departed from God's words, from Christ's commandments, from the Apostles' ordinances, from the primitive Church's examples, from the old fathers' and councils' orders, and from their own decrees, and which will be bound within the compass of none, neither old nor new, nor their own nor other folks', nor man's law nor God's law, then it is out of all question that the Romish Church hath not only had power to err, but also that it hath shamefully and most wickedly erred in very deed.

But, say they, "ye have been of our fellowship, but now ye are become forsakers of your profession, and have departed from us." It is true; we have departed from them, and for so doing we both give thanks to Almighty God, and greatly rejoice on our own behalf. But yet for all this, from the primitive Church, from the Apostles, and from Christ we have not departed. True it is, we were brought up with these men in darkness, and in the lack of the knowledge of God, as Moses was taught up in the learning and in the bosom of the Egyptians. "We have been of your company," saith Tertullian, "I confess it, and no marvel at all; for," saith he, "men be made and not born Christians." But wherefore, I pray you, have they themselves, the citizens and dwellers of Rome, removed and come down from those seven hills, whereupon Rome sometime stood, to dwell rather in the plain called Mars' field? they will say, peradventure, because the conduits of water, wherewithout men cannot commodiously live, have now failed and are dried up in those hills. Well, then, let them give us like leave in seeking the water of eternal life, that they give themselves in seeking the water of the well. For the water, verily, failed amongst them. "The elders of the Jews," saith Jeremy, "sent their little ones to the waterings; and they finding no water, being in a miserable case, and utterly marred for thirst, brought home again their vessels empty." "The needy and poor folk," saith Esay, "sought about for water, but nowhere found they any; their tongue was even withered for thirst." Even so these men have broken in pieces all the pipes and conduits: they have stopped up all the springs, and choked up the fountain of living water with dirt and mire. And as Caligula many years past locked up fast all the storehouses of corn in Rome, and thereby brought a general dearth and famine amongst the people; even so these men, by damming up all the fountains of God's Word, have brought the people into a pitiful thirst. They have brought into the world, as saith the prophet Amos, "a hunger and a thirst: not the hunger of bread, nor the thirst of water, but of hearing the Word of God." With great distress went they scattering about, seeking some spark of heavenly life to refresh their consciences withal: but that light was already thoroughly quenched out, so that they could find none. This was a rueful state; this was a lamentable form of God's Church. It was a misery to live therein, without the Gospel, without light, and without all comfort.

Wherefore, though our departing were a trouble to them, yet ought they to consider withal how just cause we had of our departure. For if they will say, it is in nowise lawful for one to leave the fellowship wherein he hath been brought up, they may as well in our names, and upon our heads, condemn both the Prophets, the Apostles, and Christ Himself. For why complain they not also of this, that Lot went quite his way out of Sodom, Abraham out of Chaldea, the Israelites out of Egypt, Christ from the Jews, and Paul from the Pharisees? For except it be possible there may be a lawful cause of departing, we see no reason why Lot, Abraham, the Israelites, Christ, and Paul, may not be accused of sects and sedition, as well as others. And if these men will needs condemn us for heretics, because we do not all things at their commandment, whom, in God's name, or what kind of men ought they themselves to be taken for, which despise the commandment of Christ, and of the Apostles? If we be schismatics because we have left them, by what name, then, shall they be called themselves, which have forsaken the Greeks, from whom they first received their faith, forsaken the primitive Church, forsaken Christ Himself, and the Apostles, even as if children should forsake their parents? For though those Greeks, who at this day profess religion, and Christ's Name, have many things corrupted amongst them, yet hold they still a great number of those things which they received from the Apostles. They have neither private masses, nor mangled sacraments, nor purgatories, nor pardons. And as for the titles of high bishops, and those glorious names, they esteem them so, as whosoever he were that would take upon him the same, and would be called either universal bishop, or the head of the universal Church, they make no doubt to call such a one both a passing proud man, a man that worketh despite against all the other bishops his brethren, and a plain heretic.

Now, then, since it is manifest, and out of all peradventure, that these men have fallen from the Greeks of whom they received the Gospel, of whom they received the faith, the true religion and the Church; what is the matter, why they will not now be called home again to the same men, as it were to their originals and first founders? And why be they afraid to take a pattern of the Apostles' and old fathers' times, as though they all had been void of understanding? Do these men, ween ye, see more, or set more by the Church of God than they did who first delivered us these things?

We truly have renounced that Church, wherein we could neither have the Word of God sincerely taught, nor the sacraments rightly administered, nor the Name of God duly called upon: which Church also themselves confess to be faulty in many points; and wherein was nothing able to stay any wise man, or one that hath consideration of his own safety. To conclude, we have forsaken the Church as it is now, not as it was in old times past, and have so gone from it as Daniel went out of the lions' den, and the three children out of the furnace: and to say the truth, we have been cast out by these men (being cursed of them as they used to say, with book, bell, and candle), rather than have gone away from them of ourselves.

And we are come to that Church, wherein they themselves cannot deny (if they will say truly, and as they think in their own conscience) but all things be governed purely and reverently, and, as much as we possibly could, very near to the order used in the old times.

Let them compare our churches and theirs together, and they shall see that themselves have most shamefully gone from the

Apostles, and we most justly have gone from them. For we, following the example of Christ, of the Apostles, and the Holy fathers, give the people the Holy Communion, whole and perfect; but these men, contrary to all the fathers, to all the Apostles, and contrary to Christ Himself, do sever the Sacraments, and pluck away the one part from the people, and that with most notorious sacrilege, as Gelasius termeth it.

We have brought again the Lord's Supper unto Christ's institution, and have made it to be a communion in very deed, common and indifferent to a great number, according to the name. But these men have changed all things contrary to Christ's institution, and have made a private mass of the Holy Communion. And so it cometh to pass that we give the Lord's Supper unto the people, and they give them a vain pageant to gaze upon.

We affirm, together with the ancient fathers, that the body of Christ is not eaten but of the good and faithful, and of those that are endued with the Spirit of Christ. Their doctrine is, that Christ's very body effectually, and as they speak really and substantially, may not only be eaten of the wicked and unfaithful men, but also (which is monstrous to be spoken) of mice and dogs.

We use to pray in our churches after that fashion, as, according to Paul's lesson, the people may know what we pray, and may answer Amen with a general consent. These men, like sounding metal, yell out in the churches unknown and strange words without understanding, without knowledge, and without devotion; yea, and do it of purpose because the people should understand nothing at all.

But not to tarry about rehearsing all points wherein we and they differ--for they have well-nigh no end--we turn the Scriptures into all tongues; they scant suffer them to be had abroad in any tongue. We allure the people to read and to hear God's Word: they drive the people from it. We desire to have our cause known to all the world; they flee to come to any trial. We lean unto knowledge, they unto ignorance. We trust unto light, they unto darkness. We reverence, as it becometh us, the writings of the Apostles and Prophets; and they burnt them. Finally, we in God's cause desire to stand to God's only judgment; they will stand only to their own. Wherefore, if they will weigh all these things with a quiet mind, and fully bent to hear and to learn, they will not only allow this determination of ours, who have forsaken errors, and followed Christ and His Apostles, but themselves also will forsake their own selves, and join of their own accord to our side.

PART VI

But peradventure they will say, it was treason to attempt these matters without a sacred general council; for in that consisteth the whole force of the Church; there Christ hath promised He will ever be a present assistant. Yet they themselves, without tarrying for any general council, have broken the commandments of God, and the decrees of the Apostles; and, as we said a little above, they have spoiled and disannulled almost all, not only ordinances, but even the doctrine of the primitive Church. And where they say it is not lawful to make a change without a council, what was he that gave us these laws, or from whence had they this injunction?

Truly, King Agesilaus did but fondly, who, when he had a determinate answer made him of the opinion and will of mighty Jupiter, would afterward bring the whole matter before Apollo, to know whether he would allow thereof, as his father Jupiter did, or no. But yet should we do much more fondly, when we hear God Himself plainly speak to us in His most Holy Scriptures, and may understand by them His will and meaning, if we would afterward (as though this were of none effect) bring our whole cause to be tried by a council; which were nothing else but to ask whether men would allow as God did, and whether men would confirm God's commandment by their authority.

Why, I beseech you, except a council will and command, shall not truth be truth, and God be God? If Christ had meant to do so from the beginning, as that He would preach or teach nothing without the bishop's consent, but refer all His doctrine over to Annas and Caiaphas, where should now have been the Christian faith? or, who at any time should have heard the Gospel taught? Peter verily, whom the Pope hath oftener in his mouth, and more reverently useth to speak of than he doth of Jesus Christ, did boldly stand against the holy council, saying, "It is better to obey God than men." And after Paul had once entirely embraced the Gospel, and had received it, "not from men, nor by man, but by the only will of God, he did not take advice therein of flesh and blood," nor brought the case before his kinsmen and brethren, but went forthwith into Arabia, to preach God's Divine mysteries by God's only authority.

Yet truly, we do not despise councils, assemblies, and conference of bishops and learned men; neither have we done that we have done altogether without bishops or without a council. The matter hath been treated in open Parliament with long consultation, and before a notable synod and convocation. But touching this council which is now summoned by the Pope Pius, wherein men so lightly are condemned, which have been neither called, heard, nor seen, it is easy to guess what we may look for or hope of it.

In times past, when Nazianzen saw in his days how men in such assemblies were so blind and wilful that they were carried with affections, and laboured more to get the victory than the truth, he pronounced openly that he never had seen any good end of any council. What would he say now, if he were alive at this day, and understood the heaving and shoving of these men? For at that time, though the matter were laboured on all sides, yet the controversies were well heard, and open error was put clean away by the general voice of all parts. But these men will neither have the case to be freely disputed, nor yet, how many errors soever there be, suffer they any to be changed. For it is a common custom of theirs often and shamelessly to boast that "their Church cannot err; that in it there is no fault; and that they must give place to us in nothing." Or if there be any fault, yet must it be tried by bishops and abbots only, because they be the directors and rulers of matters; and they be the Church of God. Aristotle saith that a "city cannot consist of bastards;" but whether the Church of God may consist of these men, let their own selves consider. For doubtless neither be the abbots legitimate abbots, nor the bishops natural right bishops. But grant they be the Church: let them be heard speak in councils; let them alone have authority to give assent: yet in old time, when the Church of God (if ye will compare it with their Church) was very well governed, both elders and deacons, as saith Cyprian, and certain also of the common people, were called thereunto, and made acquainted with ecclesiastical matters.

But I put case, these abbots [and bishops] have no knowledge: what if they understand nothing what religion is, nor how we ought to think of God? I put case, the pronouncing and ministering of the law be decayed in priests, and good counsel fail in the elders, and, as the prophet Micah saith, "The night be unto them instead of a vision, and darkness instead of prophesying:" or, as

Esaias saith, "What if all the watchmen of the city are become blind?" "What if the salt have lost his proper strength and savoriness," and, as Christ saith, "be good for no use, scant worth the casting on the dunghill?"

Well, yet then they will bring all matters before the Pope, who cannot err. To this I say, first, it is a madness to think that the Holy Ghost taketh His flight from a general council to run to Rome, to the end if He doubt or stick in any matter, and cannot expound it of Himself, He may take counsel of some other spirit, I wot not what, that is better learned than Himself. For if this be true, what needed so many bishops, with so great charges and so far journeys, have assembled their convocation at this present at Trident? It had been more wisdom and better, at least it had been a much nearer way and handsomer, to have brought all things rather before the Pope, and to have come straight forth, and have asked counsel at his divine breast. Secondly, it is also an unlawful dealing to toss our matter from so many bishops and abbots, and to bring it at last to the trial of one only man, specially of him who himself is appeached by us of heinous and foul enormities, and hath not yet put in his answer; who hath also aforehand condemned us without judgment by order pronounced, and ere ever we were called to be judged.

How say ye, do we devise these tales? Is not this the course of the councils in these days? Are not all things removed from the whole holy council, and brought before the Pope alone? that, as though nothing had been done to purpose by the judgments and consents of such a number, he alone may add, alter, diminish, disannul, allow, remit, and qualify whatsoever he list? Whose words be these, then? and why have the bishops and abbots, in the last council of Trident, but of late concluded with saying thus in the end: "Saving always the authority of the see apostolic in all things?" or why doth Pope Paschal write so proudly of himself? "As though," saith he, "there were any general council able to prescribe a law to the Church of Rome: whereas all councils both have been made and have received their force and strength by the Church of Rome's authority; and in ordinances made by councils, is ever plainly excepted the authority of the Bishop of Rome." If they will have these things allowed for good, why be councils called? But if they command them to be void, why are they left in their books as things allowable?

But be it so: let the Bishop of Rome alone be above all councils, that is to say, let some one part be greater than the whole; let him be of greater power, let him be of more wisdom than all his; and, in spite of Hierom's head, let the authority "of one city be greater than the authority of the whole world." How, then, if the Pope have seen none of these things, and have never read either the Scriptures, or the old Fathers, or yet his own councils? How if he favour the Arians, as once Pope Liberius did? or have a wicked and a detestable opinion of the life to come, and of the immortality of the soul, as Pope John had but few years since? or, to increase his own dignity, do corrupt other councils, as Pope Zosimus corrupted the council holden at Nice in times past; and do say that those things were devised and appointed by the holy Fathers which never once came into their thought; and, to have the full sway of authority, do wrest the Scriptures, which, as Camotensis saith, is an usual custom with the Popes? How if he have renounced the faith of Christ, and become an apostate, as Lyranus saith many Popes have been? And, yet for all this, shall the Holy Ghost, with turning of a hand, knock at his breast, and even whether he will or no, yea, and wholly against his will, kindle him a light so as he may not err? Shall he straightway be the head-spring of all right; and shall all treasure of wisdom and understanding be found in him, as it were laid up in store? or, if these things be not in him, can he give a right and apt judgment of so weighty matters? or, if he be not able to judge, would he have that all those matters should be brought before him alone?

What will ye say if the Pope's advocates, abbots and bishops, dissemble not the matter, but show themselves open enemies to the Gospel, and though they see, yet they will not see; but wry the Scriptures, and wittingly and knowingly corrupt and counterfeit the Word of God, and foully and wickedly apply to the Pope all the same things, which evidently and properly be spoken of the Person of Christ only, nor by no means can be applied to any other? And what though they say, "The Pope is all and above all?" or, "that he can do as much as Christ can?" and "that one judgment-place and one council-house serve for the Pope and for Christ both together;" or, "that the Pope is the same light which should come into the world;" which words Christ spake of Himself alone: and "that whoso is an evil-doer hateth and flieth from that light;" or that all the other bishops have received of the Pope's fulness? Shortly, what though they make decrees expressly against God's Word, and that not in hucker-mucker or covertly, but openly, and in the face of the world, must it needs yet be Gospel straight whatsoever these men say? Shall these be God's holy army? or will Christ be at hand among them there? Shall the Holy Ghost flow in their tongues; or can they with truth say, "We and the Holy Ghost have thought good so?" Indeed, Peter Asotus and his companion Hosius stick not to affirm, that the same council wherein our Saviour Jesus Christ was condemned to die had both the Spirit of Prophesying, and the Holy Ghost, and the Spirit of Truth in it; and that it was neither a false nor a trifling saying when those bishops said, "We have a law, and by our law He ought to die:" and that they, so saying, did light upon the very truth of judgment (for so be Hosius' words); and that the same plainly was a just decree whereby they pronounced that Christ was worthy to die. This, methinketh, is strange, that these men are not able to speak for themselves, and to defend their own cause, but they must also take part with Annas and Caiaphas. For if they will call that a lawful and a good council wherein the Son of God was most shamefully condemned to die, what council will they then allow for false and naught? And yet (as all their councils, to say truth, commonly be) necessity compelled them to pronounce these things of the council holden by Annas and Caiaphas.

But will these men (I say) reform us the Church, being themselves both the persons guilty and the judges too? Will they abate their own ambition and pride? Will they overthrow their own matter, and give sentence against themselves that they must leave off to be unlearned bishops, slow bellies, heapers together of benefices, takers upon them as princes and men of war? Will the abbots, the Pope's dear darlings, judge that monk for a thief which laboureth not for his living? and that it is against all law to suffer such a one to live and to be found either in city or in country, or yet of other men's charges? or else that a monk ought to lie on the ground, to live hardly with herbs and pease, to study earnestly, to argue, to pray, to work with hand, and fully to bend himself to come to the ministry of the Church? In faith, as soon will the Pharisees and Scribes repair again the temple of God, and restore it unto us a house of prayer instead of a thievish den.

There have been, I know, certain of their own selves which have found fault with many errors in the Church, as Pope Adrian, AEneas Sylvius, Cardinal Pole, Pighius, and others, as is aforesaid: they held afterwards their council at Trident in the selfsame place where it is now appointed. There assembled many bishops, and abbots, and others whom it behoved for that matter. They were alone by themselves; whatsoever they did, nobody gainsaid it; for they had quite shut out and barred our side from all manner of assemblies: and there they sat six years, feeding folks with a marvellous expectation of their doings. The first six months, as though it were greatly needful, they made many determinations of the Holy Trinity, of the Father, of the Son, and of the Holy Ghost, which were godly things indeed, but not so necessary for that time. Let us see, in all that while, of so many, so manifest, so often confessed by them, and so evident errors, what one error have they amended? from what kind of idolatry have they reclaimed the people? What superstition have they taken away? What piece of their tyranny and pomp have they diminished? As though all the world may not now see that this is a conspiracy and not a council; and that those bishops whom the Pope hath now called together be wholly sworn and become bound to bear him their faithful allegiance, and will do no manner of thing but that they perceive pleaseth him, and helpeth to advance his power, and as he will have it; or that they reckon not of the number of men's voices rather than have weight and consideration of the same; or that might doth not oftentimes overcome right.

And therefore we know that divers times many good men and Catholic bishops did tarry at home, and would not come when such councils were called, wherein men so apparently laboured to serve factions and to take parts, because they knew they should but lose their travail, and do no good, seeing whereunto their enemies' minds were so wholly bent. Athanasius denied to come, when he was called by the emperor to his council at Caesarea, perceiving plain he should but come among his enemies, which deadly hated him. The same Athanasius, when he came afterward to the council at Syrmium, and foresaw what would be the end by reason of the outrage and malice of his enemies, he packed up his carriage and went away immediately. John Chrysostom, although the Emperor Constantius commanded him by four sundry letters to come to the Arians' council, yet kept he himself at home still. When Maximus, the Bishop of Jerusalem, sat in the council at Palestine, the old Father Paphnutius took him by the hand, and led him out at the doors, saying, "It is not lawful for us to confer of these matters with wicked men." The bishops of the East would not come to the Syrmian council after they knew Athanasius had gotten himself thence again. Cyril called men back by letters from the council of them which were named Patropassians. Paulinus, Bishop of Triers, and many others more, refused to come to the council at Milan when they understood what a stir and rule Auxentius kept there: for they saw it was in vain to go thither, where not reason, but faction, should prevail, and where folk contended not for the truth and right judgment of the matter, but for partiality and favour.

And yet, for all those Fathers had such malicious and stiffnecked enemies, yet if they had come they should have had free speech at least in the councils. But now, sithence, none of us may be suffered so much as to sit, or once to be seen in these men's meetings, much less suffered to speak freely our mind; and seeing the Pope's legates, patriarchs, archbishops, bishops, and abbots--all being conspired together, all linked together in one kind of fault, and all bound by one oath--sit alone by themselves, and have power alone to give their consent: and, at last, when they have all done--as though they had done nothing--bring all their opinions to be judged at the will and pleasure of the Pope, being but one man, to the end he may pronounce his own sentence of himself, who ought rather to have answered to his complaint; sithence, also, the same ancient and Christian liberty, which of all right should specially be in Christian councils, is now utterly taken away from the council--for these causes, I say, wise and good men ought not to marvel at this day, though we do the like now, that they see was done in times past in like case of so many Fathers and Catholic bishops: which is, though we choose rather to sit at home, and leave our whole cause to God, than to journey thither, whereas we neither shall have place nor be able to do any good; whereas we can obtain no audience; whereas princes' ambassadors be but used as mocking-stocks; and whereas, also, we be condemned already, before trial, as though the matter were aforehand despatched and agreed upon. Nevertheless, we can bear patiently and quietly our own private wrongs. But wherefore do they shut out Christian kings and good princes from their convocation? Why do they so uncourteously, or with such spite, leave them out, and--as though they were not either Christian men, or else could not judge--will not have them made acquainted with the cause of Christian religion, nor understand the state of their own Churches?

Or if the said kings and princes happen to intermeddle in such matters, and take upon them to do that they may do, that they be commanded to do, and ought of duty to do, and the same things that we know both David and Solomon and other good princes have done, that is, if they--whilst the Pope and his prelates slug and sleep, or else mischievously withstand them--do bridle the priests' sensuality, and drive them to do their duty, and keep them still to it; if they do overthrow idols, if they take away superstition, and set up again the true worshipping of God--why do they by-and-by make an outcry upon them, that such princes trouble all, and press by violence into another body's office, and do thereby wickedly and malapertly? What Scripture hath at any time forbidden a Christian prince to be made privy to such causes? Who but themselves alone made ever any such law?

They will say to this, I guess: "Civil princes have learned to govern a commonwealth, and to order matters of war, but they understand not the secret mysteries of religion." If that be so, what is the Pope, I pray you, at this day other than a monarch or a prince? Or what be the cardinals, who must be none other nowadays, but princes and kings' sons? What else be the patriarchs, and, for the most part, the archbishops, the bishops, the abbots? What be they else at this present in the Pope's kingdom but worldly princes, but dukes and earls, gorgeously accompanied with bands of men whithersoever they go; oftentimes also gaily arrayed with chains and collars of gold? They have at times, too, certain ornaments by themselves, as crosses, pillars, hats, mitres, and palls--which pomp the ancient bishops Chrysostom, Augustine, and Ambrose never had. Setting these things aside, what teach they? What say they? What do they? How live they? I say, not as may become a bishop, but as may become even a Christian man? Is it so great a matter to have a vain title, and, by changing a garment only, to have the name of a bishop?

Surely to have the principal stay and effect of all matters committed wholly to these men's hands, who neither know nor will know these things, nor yet set a jot by any point of religion, save that which concerneth their belly and riot; and to have them alone sit as judges, and to be set up as overseers in the watch-tower, being no better than blind spies; of the other side, to have a Christian prince of good understanding and of a right judgment to stand still like a block or a stake, not to be suffered neither to give his voice nor to show his judgment, but only to wait what these men shall will and command, as one which had neither ears, nor eyes, nor wit, nor heart; and whatsoever they give in charge, to allow it without exception, blindly fulfilling their commandments, be they never so blasphemous and wicked, yea, although they command him quite to destroy all religion, and to crucify again Christ Himself: this surely, besides that it is proud and spiteful, is also beyond all right and reason, and not to be endured of Christian and wise princes. Why, I pray you, may Caiaphas and Annas understand these matters, and may not David and Ezechias do the same? Is it lawful for a cardinal, being a man of war, and delighting in blood, to have place in a council? and is it not lawful for a Christian emperor or a king? We truly grant no further liberty to our magistrates than that we know hath both been given them by the Word of God, and also been confirmed by the examples of the very best governed commonwealths. For besides that a Christian prince hath the charge of both tables committed to him by God, to the end he may understand that not temporal matters only, but also religious and ecclesiastical causes, pertain to his office: besides also that God by His prophets often and earnestly commandeth the king to cut down the groves, to break down the images and altars of idols, and to write out the book of the law for himself: and besides that the prophet Isaiah saith, "A king ought to be a patron and a nurse of the Church:" I say, besides all these things, we see by histories and by examples of the best times that good princes ever took the administration of ecclesiastical matters to pertain to their duty.

Moses, a civil magistrate, and chief guide of the people, both received from God, and delivered to the people, all the order for religion and sacrifices, and gave Aaron the bishop a vehement and sore rebuke for making the golden calf, and for suffering the corruption of religion. Joshua also, though he were none other than a civil magistrate, yet as soon as he was chosen by God, and set as a ruler over the people, he received commandments specially touching religion and the service of God. King David, when the whole religion was altogether brought out of frame by wicked king Saul, brought home again the Ark of God; that is to say, he restored religion again; and was not only amongst them himself as a counsellor and furtherer of the work, but he appointed also hymns and psalms, put in order the companies, and was the only doer in setting forth that whole solemn show, and in effect ruled the priests. King Solomon built unto the Lord the Temple which his father David had but purposed in his mind to do: and after the finishing thereof, he made a goodly oration to the people concerning religion and the service of God: he afterward displaced Abiathar the priest, and set Sadok in his place. After this, when the Temple of God was in shameful wise polluted through the naughtiness and negligence of the priests, King Hezekiah commanded the same to be cleansed from the rubble and filth, the priests to light up candles, to burn incense, and to do their Divine service according to the old and allowed custom; the same king also commanded the brazen serpent, which then the people wickedly worshipped, to be taken, down and beaten to powder. King Jehoshaphat overthrew and utterly made away the hill altars and groves; whereby he saw God's honour hindered and the people holden back with a private superstition from the ordinary Temple, which was at Jerusalem, whereto they should by order have resorted yearly from every part of the realm. King Josiah with great diligence put the priests and bishops in mind of their duties; King Joash bridled the riot and arrogancy of the priests; Jehu put to death the wicked prophets.

And to rehearse no more examples out of the old law, let us rather consider, since the birth of Christ, how the Church hath been governed in the Gospel's time. The Christian emperors in the old time appointed the councils of the bishops. Constantine called the council at Nice; Theodosius the First called the council at Constantinople; Theodosius the Second, the council at Ephesus; Martian, the council at Chalcedon; and when Ruffine the heretic had alleged for authority a council which, as he thought, should make for him, St. Hierom his adversary, to confute him, "Tell us," quod he, "what emperor commanded that council to be called." The same St. Hierom again, in his epitaph upon Paula, maketh mention of the emperor's letters which gave commandment to call the "bishops of Italy and Greece to Rome to a council." Continually for the space of five hundred years, the emperor alone appointed the ecclesiastical assemblies, and called the councils of the bishops together.

We now therefore marvel the more at the unreasonable dealing of the Bishop of Rome, who, knowing what was the emperor's right when the Church was well ordered, knowing also that it is now a common right to all princes, for so much as the kings are now fully possessed in the several parts of the whole empire, doth so without consideration assign that office alone to himself, and taketh it sufficient, in summoning a general council, to make that man that is prince of the whole world no otherwise partaker thereof than he would make his own servant. And although the modesty and mildness of the Emperor Ferdinand be so great that he can bear this wrong, because, peradventure, he understandeth not well the Pope's packing, yet ought not the Pope of his holiness to offer him that wrong, nor to claim as his own another man's right.

But hereto some will reply: The emperor, indeed, called councils at that time ye speak of, because the Bishop of Rome was not yet grown so great as he is now, but yet the emperor did not then sit together with the bishops in council, or once bare any stroke with his authority in their consultation. I answer, Nay, that it is not so; for, as witnesseth Theodoret, the Emperor Constantine sat not only together with them in the Council of Nice, but gave also advice to the bishops how it was best to try out the matter by the Apostles' and Prophets' writings, as appeareth by these his own words: "In disputation," saith he, "of matters of divinity, we have set before us to follow the doctrine of the Holy Ghost. For the Evangelists' and the Apostles' works, and the Prophets' sayings, show us sufficiently what opinion we ought to have of the will of God." The Emperor Theodosius, as saith Socrates, did not only sit amongst the bishops, but also ordered the whole arguing of the cause, and tare in pieces the heretics' books, and allowed for good the judgment of the Catholics. In the council at Chalcedon a civil magistrate condemned for heretics, by the sentence of his own mouth, the bishops Dioscorus, Juvenalis, and Thalassius, and gave judgment to put them down from their dignities in the Church. In the third council at Constantinople, Constantine, a civil magistrate, did not only sit amongst the bishops, but did also subscribe with them. "For," saith he, "we have both read and subscribed." In the second council called Arausicanum, the prince's ambassadors, being noble men born, not only spake their mind touching religion, but set to their hands also, as well as the bishops. For thus it is written in the latter end of that council: "Petrus, Marcellinus, Felix, and Liberius, being most noble men, and famous lieutenants, and captains of France, and also peers of the realm, have given their consent, and set to their hands." Further: "Syagrius, Opilio, Pantagathus, Deodatus, Cariattho, and Marcellus, men of very great honour, have subscribed." If it be so, then, that lieutenants, captains, and peers have had authority to subscribe in council, have not emperors and kings the like authority?

Truly there had been no need to handle so plain a matter as this is with so many words, and so at length, if we had not to do with those men who, for a desire they have to strive and to win the mastery, use of course to deny all things, be they never so clear--yea, the very same which they presently see and behold with their own eyes. The Emperor Justinian made a law to correct the behaviour of the clergy, and to cut short the insolency of the priests. And albeit he were a Christian and a Catholic prince, yet put he down from their papal throne two Popes, Sylverius and Vigilius, notwithstanding they were Peter's successors and Christ's vicars.

Let us see, then, such men as have authority over the bishops, such men as receive from God commandments concerning religion, such as bring home again the Ark of God, make holy hymns, oversee the priests, build the Temple, make orations touching Divine service, cleanse the temples, destroy the hill altars, burn the idols' groves, teach the priests their duties, write them out precepts how they should live, kill the wicked prophets, displace the high priests, call together the councils of bishops, sit together with the bishops, instructing them what they ought to do, condemn and punish an heretical bishop, be made acquainted with matters of religion, which subscribe and give sentence; and do all these things, not by any other man's commission, but in their own name, and that both uprightly and godly: shall we say it pertaineth not to such men to have to do with religion? or shall we say a Christian magistrate, which dealeth amongst others in these matters, doth either naughtily, or presumptuously, or wickedly? The most ancient and Christian emperors and kings that ever were, did busy themselves with these matters, and yet were they never for this cause noted either of wickedness or of presumption. And what is he that can find out either more Catholic princes or more notable examples?

Wherefore, if it were lawful for them to do thus, being but civil magistrates, and having the chief rule of commonweals, what offence have our princes at this day made, which may not have leave to do the like, being in the like degree? or what especial gift of learning, or of judgment, or of holiness have these men now, that, contrary to the custom of all the ancient and Catholic bishops, who used to confer with princes and peers concerning religion, they do now thus reject and cast off Christian princes from knowing of the cause, and from their meetings? Well, thus doing, they wisely and warily provide for themselves and for their kingdom, which otherwise they see is like shortly to come to nought. For if so be they whom God hath placed in greatest dignity did see and perceive these men's practices, how Christ's commandments be despised by them, how the light of the Gospel is darkened and quenched out by them, and how themselves also be subtly beguiled and mocked, and unawares be deluded by them, and the way to the kingdom of heaven stopped up before them: no doubt they would never so quietly suffer themselves neither to be disdained after such a proud sort, nor so despitefully to be scorned and abused by them. But now, through their own lack of understanding, and through their own blindness, these men have them fast yoked, and in their danger.

We truly for our parts, as we have said, have done nothing in altering religion either upon rashness or arrogancy; nor nothing but with good leisure and great consideration. Neither had we ever intended to do it, except both the manifest and most assured will of God, opened to us in His Holy Scriptures, and the regard of our own salvation, had even constrained us thereunto. For though we have departed from that Church which these men call Catholic, and by that means get us envy amongst them that want skill to judge, yet is this enough for us, and ought to be enough for every wise and good man, and one that maketh account of everlasting life, that we have gone from that Church which had power to err: which Christ, who cannot err, told so long before it should err; and which we ourselves did evidently see with our eyes to have gone both from the holy fathers, and from the Apostles, and from Christ His own self, and from the primitive and Catholic Church; and we are come as near as we possibly could to the Church of the Apostles and of the old Catholic bishops and fathers; which Church we know hath hereunto been sound and perfect, and, as Tertullian termeth it, a pure virgin, spotted as yet with no idolatry, nor with any foul or shameful fault: and have directed, according to their customs and ordinances, not only our doctrine, but also the Sacraments and the form of common prayer.

And, as we know both Christ Himself and all good men heretofore have done, we have called home again to the original and first foundation that religion which hath been foully foreslowed, and utterly corrupted by these men. For we thought it meet thence to take the pattern of reforming religion from whence the ground of religion was first taken: because this one reason, as saith the most ancient father Tertullian, hath great force against all heresies, "Look, whatsoever was first, that is true; and whatsoever is latter, that is corrupt." Irenaeus oftentimes appealed to the oldest churches, which had been nearest to Christ's time, and which it was hard to believe had erred. But why at this day is not the same respect and consideration had? Why return we not to the pattern of the old churches? Why may not we hear at this time amongst us the same saying, which was openly pronounced in times past in the council at Nice by so many bishops and Catholic fathers, and nobody once speaking against it [Greek text]: that is to say, "hold still the old customs!" When Esdras went about to repair the ruins of the Temple of God, he sent not to Ephesus, although the most beautiful and gorgeous temple of Diana was there; and when he purposed to restore the sacrifices and ceremonies of God, he sent not to Rome, although peradventure he had heard in that place were the solemn sacrifices called Hecatombae, and other called Solitaurilia, Lectisternia, and Supplicationes, and Numa Pompilius' ceremonial books. He thought it enough for him to set before his eyes, and follow the pattern of the old Temple, which Solomon at the beginning builded according as God had appointed him, and also those old customs and ceremonies which God Himself had written out by special words for Moses.

The prophet Aggaeus, after the temple was repaired again by Esdras, and the people might think they had a very just cause to rejoice on their own behalf for so great a benefit received of Almighty God, yet made he them all burst out into tears, because that they which were yet alive and had seen the former building of the Temple, before the Babylonians destroyed it, called to mind how far off it was yet from that beauty and excellency which it had in the old times past before. For then, indeed, would they have thought the Temple worthily repaired if it had answered to the ancient pattern and to the majesty of the first Temple. Paul, because he would amend the abuse of the Lord's Supper, which the Corinthians even then began to corrupt, he set before them Christ's institution to follow, saying: "I have delivered unto you that which I first received of the Lord." And when Christ did confute the error of the Pharisees, "Ye must," saith He, "return to the first beginning; for from the beginning it was not thus." And when He found great fault with the priests for their uncleanness of life and covetousness, and would cleanse the Temple from all evil abuses, "This house," saith He, "at the first beginning it was a house of prayer," wherein all the people might devoutly and sincerely pray together. And so it were your part to use it now also at this day, for it was not builded to the end it should be a "den of thieves." Likewise all the good and commendable princes mentioned of in the Scriptures were praised specially by these words, that they had walked in the ways of their father David: that is, because they had returned to the first and original foundation, and had restored religion even to the perfection wherein David left it. And therefore, when we likewise saw all things were quite trodden under foot of these men, and that nothing remained in the temple of God but pitiful spoils and decays, we reckoned it the wisest and the safest way to set before our eyes those churches which we know for a surety that they never had erred, nor never had private mass, nor prayers in a strange and barbarous language, nor this corrupting of sacraments, and other toys.

And forsomuch as our desire was to have the Temple of the Lord restored anew, we would seek none other foundation than the same which we know was long ago laid by the Apostles, that is to wit, "Our Saviour, Jesus Christ." And forasmuch as we heard God Himself speaking unto us in His word, and saw also the notable examples of the old and primitive Church; again, how uncertain a matter it was to wait for a general council, and that the success thereof would be much more uncertain, but specially forsomuch as we were most ascertained of God's will, and counted it a wickedness to be too careful and overcumbered about the judgments of mortal men: we could no longer stand taking advice with flesh and blood, but rather thought good to do the same thing, that both might rightly be done, and hath also many a time been done, as well of good men as of many Catholic bishops--that is, to remedy our own churches by a provincial synod. For thus know we the old fathers used to put in experience before they came to the public universal council. There remain yet at this day canons written in councils of free cities, as of Carthage under Cyprian, as of Ancyra, Neocaesarea, and Gangra, which is in Paphlagonia, as some think, before that the name of the general council at Nice was ever heard of. After this fashion in old time did they speedily meet with and cut short those heretics, the Pelagians and the Donatists at home, by private disputation, without any general council. Thus, also, when the Emperor Constantine evidently and earnestly took part with Auxentius, the bishop of the Arians' faction, Ambrose, the bishop of the Christians, appealed not unto a general council, where he saw no good could be done, by reason of the emperor's might and great labour, but appealed to his own clergy and people, that is to say, to a provincial synod. And thus it was decreed in the council at Nice that the bishops should assemble twice every year. And in the council at Carthage it was decreed that the bishops should meet together in each of their provinces at least once in the year, which was done, as saith the council of Chalcedon, of purpose that if any errors and abuses had happened to spring up anywhere, they might immediately at the first entry be destroyed where they first began. So likewise when Secundus and Palladius rejected the council at Aquileia, because it was not a general and a common council, Ambrose, bishop of Milan, made answer that no man ought to take it for a new or strange matter that the bishops of the west part of the world did call together synods, and make private assemblies in their provinces, for that it was a thing before then used by the west bishops no few times, and by the bishops of Greece used oftentimes and commonly to be done. And so Charles the Great, being emperor, held a provincial council in Germany for putting away images, contrary to the second council at Nice. Neither, pardy, even amongst us is this so very a strange and new a trade. For we have had ere now in England provincial synods, and governed our churches by home-made laws. What should one say more? Of a truth, even those greatest councils, and where most assembly of people ever was (whereof these men use to make such an exceeding reckoning), compare them with all the churches which throughout the world acknowledge and profess the name of Christ, and what else, I pray you, can they seem to be but certain private councils of bishops and provincial synods? For admit, peradventure, Italy, France, Spain, England, Germany, Denmark, and Scotland meet together, if there want Asia, Greece, Armenia, Persia, Media, Mesopotamia, Egypt, Ethiopia, India, and Mauritania, in all which places there be both many Christian men and also bishops, how can any man, being in his right mind, think such a council to be a general council? or where so many parts of the world do lack how can they truly say they have the consent of the whole world? Or what manner of council, ween you, was the same last at Trident? Or how might it be termed a general council, when out of all Christian kingdoms and nations there came unto it but only forty bishops, and of the same some so cunning that they might be thought meet to be sent home again to learn their grammar, and so well learned that they had never studied divinity.

Whatsoever it be, the truth of the Gospel of Jesus Christ dependeth not upon councils, nor, as St. Paul saith, upon mortal creature's judgment. And if they which ought to be careful for God's Church will not be wise, but slack their duty, and harden their hearts against God and His Christ, going on still to pervert the right ways of the Lord, God will stir up the very stones, and make children and babes cunning, whereby there may ever be some to confute these men's lies. For God is able (not only without councils), but also, will the councils, nill the councils, to maintain and advance His own kingdom. "Full many be the thoughts of man's heart" (saith Solomon); "but the counsel of the Lord abideth steadfast:" "There is no wisdom, there is no knowledge, there is no counsel against the Lord." "Things endure not" (saith Hilarius), "that be set up with men's workmanship: by another manner of means must the Church of God be builded and preserved: for that Church is grounded upon the foundation of the Apostles and Prophets, and is holden fast together by one corner stone, which is Christ Jesu."

But marvellous notable, and to very good purpose for these days, be Hierom's words: "Whosoever" (saith he) "the devil hath deceived, and enticed to fall asleep, as it were with the sweet and deathly enchantments of the mermaids the Syrens, those persons doth God's word awake up, saying unto them, Arise, thou that sleepest; lift up thyself, and Christ shall give thee light. Therefore, at the coming of Christ, of God's word, of the ecclesiastical doctrine, and of the full destruction of Nineveh, and of that most beautiful harlot, then, then shall the people, which heretofore had been cast in a trance under their masters, be raised up, and shall make haste to go to the mountains of the Scripture; and there shall they find hills, Moses verily, and Joshua the son of Nun, other hills also, which are the Prophets; and hills of the New Testament, which are the Apostles and the Evangelists. And when the people shall flee for succour to such hills, and shall be exercised in the reading of those kind of mountains, though they find not one to teach them (for the harvest shall be great, but the labourers few), yet shall the good desire of the people be well accepted, in that they have gotten them to such hills; and the negligence of their masters shall be openly reproved." These be Hierom's sayings, and that so plain, as there needeth no interpreter. For they agree so just with the things we now see with our eyes have already come to pass, that we may verily think that he meant to foretell, as it were, by the spirit of prophecy, and to paint before our face the universal state of our time; the fall of the most gorgeous harlot Babylon; the repairing again of God's Church; the blindness and sloth of the bishops, and the good will and forwardness of the people. For who is so blind, that he seeth not these men be the masters, by whom the people, as saith Hierom, hath been led into error and lulled asleep? Or who sooth not Rome, that is their Nineveh, which sometime was painted with fairest colours, but now, her vizard being palled off, is both better seen and less set by? Or who seeth not that good men, being awaked, as it were, out of their dead sleep at the light of the Gospel and at the voice of God, have resorted to the hills of the Scriptures, waiting not at all for the councils of such masters?

But, by your favour, some will say, these things ought not to have been attempted without the Bishop of Rome's commandment, forsomuch as he only is the knot and band of Christian society. He only is that priest of Levi's order whom God signified in the Deuteronomy, from whom counsel in matters of weight and true judgment ought to be fetched; and whoso obeyeth not his judgment, the same man ought to be killed in the sight of his brethren; and that no mortal creature hath authority to be judge over him, whatsoever he do: that Christ reigneth in heaven, and he in earth; that he alone can do as much as Christ or God Himself can do, because Christ and he have but one council-house; that without him is no faith, no hope, no Church; and whoso goeth from him quite casteth away and renounceth his own salvation. Such talk have the canonists, the Pope's parasites, surely, but with small discretion or soberness. For they could scant say more, at least they could not speak more highly of Christ Himself.

As for us, truly we have fallen from the Bishop of Rome upon no manner of worldly respect or commodity. And would to Christ he so behaved himself as this falling away needed not; but so the case stood, that unless we left him we could not come to Christ. Neither will he now make any other league with us than such a one as Nahas the king of the Ammonites would have made in times past with them of the city of Jabez, which was to put out the right eye of each one of the inhabitants. Even so will the Pope pluck from us the holy Scripture, the Gospel of our salvation, and all the confidence which we have in Christ Jesu. And upon other condition can he not agree upon peace with us.

For whereas some use to make so great a vaunt, that the Pope is only Peter's successor, as though thereby he carried the Holy Ghost in his bosom, and cannot err, this is but a matter of nothing, and a very trifling tale. God's grace is promised to a good mind, and to one that feareth God, not unto sees and successions. "Riches," saith Hierom, "may make a bishop to be of more might than the rest: but all the bishops," whosoever they be, "are the successors of the Apostles." If so be the place and consecrating only be sufficient, why then Manasses succeeded David, and Caiaphas succeeded Aaron. And it hath been often seen, that an idol hath stand in the temple of God. In old time Archidamus the Lacedaemonian boasted much of himself, how he came of the blood of Hercules. But one Nicostratus in this wise abated his pride: "Nay," quoth he, "thou seemest not to descend from Hercules. For Hercules destroyed ill men, but thou makest good men evil." And when the Pharisees bragged of their lineage, how they were of the kindred and blood of Abraham: "Ye," saith Christ, "seek to kill me, a man which have told you the truth, as I heard it from God. Thus Abraham never did. Ye are of your father the devil, and will needs obey his will."

Yet notwithstanding, because we will grant somewhat to succession, tell us, hath the Pope alone succeeded Peter? And wherein, I pray you? In what religion? in what office? in what piece of his life hath he succeeded him? What one thing (tell me) had Peter ever like unto the Pope, or the Pope like unto Peter? Except peradventure they will say thus: that Peter, when he was at Rome, never taught the Gospel, never fed the flock, took away the keys of the kingdom of heaven, hid the treasures of his Lord, sat him down only in his castle in S. John Lateran, and pointed out with his finger all the places of purgatory, and kinds of punishments, committing some poor souls to be tormented, and other some again suddenly releasing thence at his own pleasure, taking money for so doing: or that he gave order to say private masses in every corner: or that he mumbled up the holy service with a low voice, and in an unknown language: or that he hanged up the Sacrament in every temple, and on every altar, and carried the same about before him whithersoever he went, upon an ambling jannet, with lights and bells; or that he consecrated with his holy breath, oil, wax, wool, bells, chalices, churches, and altars, or that he sold jubilees, graces, liberties, advowsons, preventions, first fruits, palls, the wearing of palls, bulls, indulgences, and pardons; or that he called himself by the name of the head of the Church, the highest bishop, bishop of bishops, alone most holy: or that by usurping he took upon himself the right and authority over other folk's churches; or that he exempted himself from the power of any civil government; or that he maintained wars, and set princes together at variance: or that he sitting in his chair, with his triple crown full of labels, with sumptuous and Persian-like gorgeousness, with his royal sceptre, with his diadem of gold, and glittering with stones, was carried about, not upon palfrey, but upon the shoulders of noble men. These things, no doubt, did Peter at Rome in times past, and left them in charge to his successors, as you would say, from hand to hand; for these things be now-a-days done at Rome by the popes, and be so done, as though nothing else ought to be done. Or contrariwise, peradventure they had rather say thus, that the Pope doth now all the same things, which we know Peter did many a day ago: that is, that he runneth up and down into every country to preach the gospel, not only openly abroad, but also privately from house to house: that he is diligent, and applieth that business in season and out of season, in due time and out of due time: that he doth the part of an evangelist, that he fulfilleth the work and ministry of Christ, that he is the watchman of the House of Israel, receiveth answers and words at God's mouth; and even as he receiveth them, so delivereth them over to the people: that he is the salt of the earth:

that he is the light of the world: that he doth not feed his own self, but his flock: that he doth not entangle himself with the worldly cares of this life: that he doth not use a sovereignty over the Lord's people: that he seeketh not to have other men minister to him, but himself rather to minister unto others: that he taketh all bishops as his fellows and equals; that he is subject to princes, as to persons sent from God: that he giveth to Caesar that which is Caesar's: and that he, as the old bishops of Rome did without any question, calleth the emperor his lord. Unless, therefore, the popes do the like now-a-days, and Peter did the things aforesaid, there is no cause at all why they should glory so of Peter's name, and of his succession.

Much less cause have they to complain of our departing, and to call us again to be fellows and friends with them, and to believe as they believe. Men say, that one Cobilon, a Lacedaemonian, when he was sent ambassador to the king of the Persians to treat of a league, and found by chance them of the court playing at dice, he returned straightway home again, leaving his message undone. And when he was asked why he did slack to do the things which he had received by public commission to do, he made answer, he thought it should be a great reproach to his commonwealth to make a league with dicers. But if we should content ourselves to return to the Pope, and to his popish errors, and to make a covenant not only with dicers, but also with men far more ungracious and wicked than any dicers be; besides that this should be a great blot to our good name, it should also be a very dangerous matter, both to kindle God's wrath against us, and to clog and condemn our own souls for ever. For of very truth we have departed from him, who we saw had blinded the whole world this many a hundred year: from him, who too far presumptuously was wont to say, "he could not err," and whatsoever he did "no mortal man had power to condemn him, neither kings, nor emperors, nor the whole clergy," nor yet all the people in the world together; no, and though he should carry away with him to hell a thousand souls from him who took upon him power to command, not only men, but even God's angels, to go, to return, to lead souls into purgatory, and to bring them back again when he list himself: whom Gregory said, without all doubt, is the very forerunner and standard-bearer of Antichrist, and hath utterly forsaken the Catholic faith, from whom also these ringleaders of ours, who now with might and main resist the gospel, and the truth, which they know to be the truth, have ere this departed every one of their own accord and goodwill, and would even now also gladly depart from him, if the note of inconstancy and shame, and their own estimation among the people, were not a let unto them. In conclusion, we have departed from him, to whom we were not bound, and who had nothing to say for himself, but only I know not what virtue or power of the place where he dwelleth, and a continuance of succession.

And as for us, we of all others most justly have left him. For our kings, yea, even they which with greatest reverence did follow and obey the authority and faith of the bishops of Rome, have long since found and felt well enough the yoke and tyranny of the Pope's kingdom. For the bishops of Rome took the crown off from the head of our King Henry the Second, and compelled him to put aside all majesty, and like a mere private man to come unto their legate with great submission and humility, so as all his subjects might laugh him to scorn. More than this, they caused bishops and monks, and some part of the nobility, to be in the field against our King John, and set all the people at liberty from their oaths, whereby they ought allegiance to their king; and at last, wickedly and most abominably they bereaved the king, not only of his kingdom, but also of his life. Besides this, they excommunicated and cursed king Henry the Eighth, that most famous prince, and stirred up against him, sometime the Emperor, sometime the French king: and as much as in them was, put in adventure our realm to have been a very prey and spoil. Yet were they but fools and mad, to think that either so mighty a prince could be scared with bugs and rattles; or else, that so noble and great a kingdom might so easily, even at one morsel, be devoured and swallowed up.

And yet, as though all this were too little, they would needs make all the realm tributary to them, and exacted thence yearly most unjust and wrongful taxes. So dear cost us the friendship of the city of Rome. Wherefore, if they have gotten these things of us by extortion, through their fraud and subtle sleights, we see no reason why we may not pluck away the same from them again by lawful ways and just means. And if our kings in that darkness and blindness of former times, gave them these things of their own accord and liberality for religion's sake, being moved with a certain opinion of their feigned holiness; now when ignorance and error is espied out, may the kings, their successors, take them away again, seeing they have the same authority the kings their ancestors had before. For the gift is void, except it be hallowed by the will of the giver, and that cannot seem a perfect will, which is dimmed and hindered by error.

THE RECAPITULATION OF THE APOLOGY

Thus, good Christian reader, ye see how it is no new thing, though at this day the religion of Christ be entertained with despites and checks, being but lately restored, and as it were, coming up again anew; forsomuch as the like hath chanced both to Christ Himself and to His Apostles: yet nevertheless, for fear ye may suffer yourself to be led amiss and seduced with these exclamations of our adversaries, we have declared at large unto you the very whole manner of our religion, what our opinion is of God the Father, of His only Son Jesus Christ, of the Holy Ghost, of the Church, of the Sacraments, of the ministry, of the Scriptures, of ceremonies, and of every part of Christian belief. We have said, that we abandon and detest, as plagues and poisons, all those old heresies which either the sacred Scriptures, or the ancient councils have utterly condemned: that we call home again, as much as ever we can, the right discipline of the Church, which our adversaries have quite brought into a poor and weak case. That we punish all licentiousness of life, and unruliness of manners, by the old and long-continued laws, and with as much sharpness as is convenient, and lieth in our power. That we maintain still the state of kingdoms, in the same condition and plight wherein we have found them, without any diminishing or alteration, reserving unto our princes their majesties and worldly pre-eminence, safe and without impairing, to our possible power. That we have so gotten ourselves away from that Church, which they had made a den of thieves, and wherein nothing was in good frame, or once like to the Church of God, and which, themselves confessed, had erred many ways, even as Lot in times past gat him out of Sodom, or Abraham out of Chaldea, not upon a desire of contention, but by the warning of God Himself. And that we have searched out of the Holy Bible, which we are sure cannot deceive, one sure form of religion, and have returned again unto the primitive Church of the ancient fathers and Apostles; that is to say, to the first ground and beginning of things, as unto the very foundations and headsprings of Christ's Church. And in very truth we have not tarried for in this matter the authority or consent of the Tridentine council, wherein we saw nothing done uprightly, nor by good order; where also everybody was sworn to the maintenance of one man; where our prince's ambassadors were contemned; where not one of our divines could be heard, and where parts-taking and ambition was openly and earnestly procured and wrought; but, as the holy fathers in former time, and as our predecessors have commonly done, we have restored our churches by a provincial convocation, and have clean shaken off, as our duty was, the yoke and tyranny of the bishop of Rome, to whom we were not bound; who also had no manner of thing like, neither to Christ, nor to Peter, nor to an Apostle, nor yet like to any bishop at all. Finally, we say, that we agree amongst ourselves touching the whole judgment and chief substance of Christian religion, and with one mouth, and with one spirit, do worship God, and the Father of our Lord Jesus Christ.

Wherefore, O Christian and godly reader, forasmuch as thou seest the reasons and causes, both why we have restored religion, and why we have forsaken these men, thou oughtest not to marvel, though we have chosen to obey our Master Christ, rather than men. Paul hath given us warning how we should not suffer ourselves to be carried away with such sundry learnings, and to fly their companies, in especial, which would sow debate and variances, clean contrary to the doctrine which they had received of Christ and the Apostles. Long since have these men's crafts and treacheries decayed, and vanished, and fled away at the sight and light of the Gospel, even as the owl doth at the sun-rising. And albeit their trumpery be built up, and reared as high as the sky, yea even, in a moment, and as it were of the own self, falleth it down again to the ground and cometh to nought. For you must not think that all these things have come to pass rashly, or at adventure; it hath been God's pleasure, that, against all men's wills well nigh, the Gospel of Jesu Christ should be spread abroad throughout the whole world at these days. And, therefore, men, following God's biddings, have of their own free will resorted unto the doctrine of Jesus Christ. And for our parts, truly we have sought hereby, neither glory, nor wealth, nor pleasure, nor ease. For there is plenty of all these things with our adversaries. And when we were of their side, we enjoyed such worldly commodities much more liberally and bountifully than we do now. Neither do we eschew concord and peace, but to have peace with man we will not be at war with God. The name of peace is a sweet and pleasant thing, saith Hilarius; but yet beware, saith he, "peace is one thing, and bondage is another." For if it should so be, as they seek to have it, that Christ should be commanded to keep silence, that the truth of the Gospel should be betrayed, that horrible errors should be cloaked, that Christian men's eyes should be bleared, and that they might be suffered to conspire openly against God; this were not a peace, but a most ungodly covenant of servitude. There is a peace, saith Nazianzen, that is unprofitable; again, there is a discord, saith he, that is profitable. For we must conditionally desire peace, so far as is lawful before God, and so far as we may conveniently. For otherwise Christ Himself brought not peace into the world, but a sword. Wherefore, if the pope will have us be reconciled to him, his duty is first to be reconciled to God. For from thence, saith Cyprian, spring schisms and sects, because men seek not the Head, and have not their recourse to the fountain (of the Scriptures), and keep not the rules given by the heavenly Teacher. For, saith he, that is not peace, but war; neither is he joined unto the Church, which is severed from the Gospel. As for these men, they used to make a merchandise of the name of peace. For that peace which they so fain would have, is only a rest of idle bellies. They and we might easily be brought to atonement; touching all these matters, were it not that ambition, gluttony, and excess did let it. Hence cometh their whining, their heart is on their halfpenny. Out of doubt their clamours and stirs be to none other end, but to maintain more shamefully and naughtily ill-gotten things.

Nowadays the pardoners complain of us, the dataries, the pope's collectors, the bawds, and others which take gain to be godliness, and serve not Jesus Christ but their own bellies. Many a day ago, and in the old world, a wonderful great advantage grew hereby to these kinds of people. But now they reckon, all is lost unto them, that Christ gaineth. The pope himself maketh a great complaint at this present, that charity in people is waxen cold. And why so, trow ye? Forsooth, because his profits decay more and more. And for this cause doth he hale us into hatred, all that ever he may, laying load upon us with despiteful railings, and condemning us for heretics, to the end, they that understand not the matter may think there be no worse men upon earth than we be. Notwithstanding, we in the mean season are never the more ashamed for all this; neither ought we to be ashamed of the gospel. For we set more by the glory of God, than we do by the estimation of men. We are sure all is true that we teach, and we may not either go against our own conscience, or bear any witness against God. For if we deny any part of the Gospel of Jesus Christ before men, He on the other side will deny us before His Father. And if there be any that will still be offended, and cannot endure Christ's doctrine, such, say we, be blind, and leaders of the blind; the truth, nevertheless, must be preached and preferred above all, and we must with patience wait for God's judgment. Let these folk, in the meantime, take good heed what they do, and let them be well advised of their own salvation, and cease to hate and persecute the Gospel of the Son of God, for fear lest they feel Him once a redresser and revenger of His own cause. God will not suffer Himself to be made a mocking stock. The world espieth a good while agone what there is a doing abroad. This flame, the more it is kept down, so much the more with greater force and strength doth it break out and fly abroad. Their unfaithfulness shall not disappoint God's faithful promise. And if they shall refuse to lay away this their hardness of heart, and to receive the Gospel of Christ, then shall publicans and sinners go before them into the kingdom of Heaven.

God and the Father of our Lord Jesus Christ open the eyes of them all, that they may be able to see that blessed hope, whereunto they have been called; so as we may altogether in one glorify Him alone, who is the true God, and also that same Jesus Christ, whom He sent down to us from Heaven, unto whom, with the Father and the Holy Ghost, be given all honour and glory everlastingly. So be it.

THE END

www.bookjungle.com *email: sales@bookjungle.com fax: 630-214-0564 mail: Book Jungle PO Box 2226 Champaign, IL 61825*

The Two Babylons
Alexander Hislop

You may be surprised to learn that many traditions of Roman Catholicism in fact don't come from Christ's teachings but from an ancient Babylonian "Mystery" religion that was centered on Nimrod, his wife Semiramis, and a child Tammuz. This book shows how this ancient religion transformed itself as it incorporated Christ into its teachings....

Religion/History **Pages:358** QTY

ISBN: ***1-59462-010-5*** *MSRP* ***$22.95***

The Go-Getter
Kyne B. Peter

The Go Getter is the story of William Peck.He was a war veteran and amputee who will not be refused what he wants. Peck not only fights to find employment but continually proves himself more than competent at the many difficult test that are throw his way in the course of his early days with the Ricks Lumber Company...

Business/Self Help/Inspirational **Pages:68** QTY

ISBN: ***1-59462-186-1*** *MSRP* ***$8.95***

The Power Of Concentration
Theron Q. Dumont

It is of the utmost value to learn how to concentrate. To make the greatest success of anything you must be able to concentrate your entire thought upon the idea you are working on. The person that is able to concentrate utilizes all constructive thoughts and shuts out all destructive ones...

Self Help/Inspirational **Pages:196**

ISBN: ***1-59462-141-1*** *MSRP* ***$14.95***

Self Mastery
Emile Coue

Emile Coue came up with novel way to improve the lives of people. He was a pharmacist by trade and often saw ailing people. This lead him to develop autosuggestion, a form of self-hypnosis. At the time his theories weren't popular but over the years evidence is mounting that he was indeed right all along...

New Age/Self Help **Pages:98**

ISBN: ***1-59462-189-6*** *MSRP* ***$7.95***

Rightly Dividing The Word
Clarence Larkin

The "Fundamental Doctrines" of the Christian Faith are clearly outlined in numerous books on Theology, but they are not available to the average reader and were mainly written for students. The Author has made it the work of his ministry to preach the "Fundamental Doctrines." To this end he has aimed to express them in the simplest and clearest manner..

Religion **Pages:352**

ISBN: ***1-59462-334-1*** *MSRP* ***$23.45***

The Awful Disclosures Of Maria Monk

"I cannot banish the scenes and characters of this book from my memory. To me it can never appear like an amusing fable, or lose its interest and importance. The story is one which is continually before me, and must return fresh to my mind with painful emotions as long as I live..."

Religion **Pages:232**

ISBN: ***1-59462-160-8*** *MSRP* ***$17.95***

The Law of Psychic Phenomena
Thomson Jay Hudson

"I do not expect this book to stand upon its literary merits; for if it is unsound in principle, felicity of diction cannot save it, and if sound, homeliness of expression cannot destroy it. My primary object in offering it to the public is to assist in bringing Psychology within the domain of the exact sciences. That this has never been accomplished..."

New Age **Pages:420**

ISBN: ***1-59462-124-1*** *MSRP* ***$29.95***

As a Man Thinketh
James Allen

"This little volume (the result of meditation and experience) is not intended as an exhaustive treatise on the much-written-upon subject of the power of thought. It is suggestive rather than explanatory, its object being to stimulate men and women to the discovery and perception of the truth that by virtue of the thoughts which they choose and encourage..."

Inspirational/Self Help **Pages:80**

ISBN: ***1-59462-231-0*** *MSRP* ***$9.45***

Beautiful Joe
Marshall Saunders

When Marshall visited the Moore family in 1892, she discovered Joe, a dog they had nursed back to health from his previous abusive home to live a happy life. So moved was she, that she wrote this classic masterpiece which won accolades and was recognized as a heartwarming symbol for humane animal treatment...

Fiction **Pages:256**

ISBN: ***1-59462-261-2*** *MSRP* ***$18.45***

The Enchanted April
Elizabeth Von Arnim

It began in a woman's club in London on a February afternoon, an uncomfortable club, and a miserable afternoon when Mrs. Wilkins, who had come down from Hampstead to shop and had lunched at her club, took up The Times from the table in the smoking-room...

Fiction **Pages:368**

ISBN: ***1-59462-150-0*** *MSRP* ***$23.45***

The Codes Of Hammurabi And Moses - W. W. Davies

The discovery of the Hammurabi Code is one of the greatest achievements of archaeology, and is of paramount interest, not only to the student of the Bible, but also to all those interested in ancient history...

Religion **Pages:132**

ISBN: ***1-59462-338-4*** *MSRP* ***$12.95***

Holland - The History Of Netherlands
Thomas Colley Grattan

Thomas Grattan was a prestigious writer from Dublin who served as British Consul to the US. Among his works is an authoritative look at the history of Holland. A colorful and interesting look at history....

History/Politics **Pages:408**

ISBN: ***1-59462-137-3*** *MSRP* ***$26.95***

The Thirty-Six Dramatic Situations
Georges Polti

An incredibly useful guide for aspiring authors and playwrights. This volume categorizes every dramatic situation which could occur in a story and describes them in a list of 36 situations. A great aid to help inspire or formalize the creative writing process...

Self Help/Reference **Pages:204**

ISBN: ***1-59462-134-9*** *MSRP* ***$15.95***

A Concise Dictionary of Middle English
A. L. Mayhew
Walter W. Skeat

The present work is intended to meet, in some measure, the requirements of those who wish to make some study of Middle-English, and who find a difficulty in obtaining such assistance as will enable them to find out the meanings and etymologies of the words most essential to their purpose...

Reference/History **Pages:332**

ISBN: ***1-59462-119-5*** *MSRP* ***$29.95***

www.bookjungle.com *email: sales@bookjungle.com fax: 630-214-0564 mail: Book Jungle PO Box 2226 Champaign, IL 61825*

www.bookjungle.com *email: sales@bookjungle.com fax: 630-214-0564 mail: Book Jungle PO Box 2226 Champaign, IL 61825*

QTY

The Rosicrucian Cosmo-Conception Mystic Christianity *by* ***Max Heindel*** **ISBN:** ***1-59462-188-8*** **$38.95**
The Rosicrucian Cosmo-conception is not dogmatic, neither does it appeal to any other authority than the reason of the student. It is: not controversial, but is: sent forth in the, hope that it may help to clear... *New Age/Religion Pages 646*

Abandonment To Divine Providence *by* ***Jean-Pierre de Caussade*** **ISBN:** ***1-59462-228-0*** **$25.95**
"The Rev. Jean Pierre de Caussade was one of the most remarkable spiritual writers of the Society of Jesus in France in the 18th Century. His death took place at Toulouse in 1751. His works have gone through many editions and have been republished... *Inspirational/Religion Pages 400*

Mental Chemistry *by* ***Charles Haanel*** **ISBN:** ***1-59462-192-6*** **$23.95**
Mental Chemistry allows the change of material conditions by combining and appropriately utilizing the power of the mind. Much like applied chemistry creates something new and unique out of careful combinations of chemicals the mastery of mental chemistry... *New Age Pages 354*

The Letters of Robert Browning and Elizabeth Barret Barrett 1845-1846 vol II **ISBN:** ***1-59462-193-4*** **$35.95**
by ***Robert Browning*** *and* ***Elizabeth Barrett*** *Biographies Pages 596*

Gleanings In Genesis (volume I) *by* ***Arthur W. Pink*** **ISBN:** ***1-59462-130-6*** **$27.45**
Appropriately has Genesis been termed "the seed plot of the Bible" for in it we have, in germ form, almost all of the great doctrines which are afterwards fully developed in the books of Scripture which follow... *Religion/Inspirational Pages 420*

The Master Key *by* ***L. W. de Laurence*** **ISBN:** ***1-59462-001-6*** **$30.95**
In no branch of human knowledge has there been a more lively increase of the spirit of research during the past few years than in the study of Psychology, Concentration and Mental Discipline. The requests for authentic lessons in Thought Control, Mental Discipline and... *New Age/Business Pages 422*

The Lesser Key Of Solomon Goetia *by* ***L. W. de Laurence*** **ISBN:** ***1-59462-092-X*** **$9.95**
This translation of the first book of the "Lernegton" which is now for the first time made accessible to students of Talismanic Magic was done, after careful collation and edition, from numerous Ancient Manuscripts in Hebrew, Latin, and French... *New Age/Occult Pages 92*

Rubaiyat Of Omar Khayyam *by* ***Edward Fitzgerald*** **ISBN:***1-59462-332-5* **$13.95**
Edward Fitzgerald, whom the world has already learned, in spite of his own efforts to remain within the shadow of anonymity, to look upon as one of the rarest poets of the century, was born at Bredfield, in Suffolk, on the 31st of March, 1809. He was the third son of John Purcell... *Music Pages 172*

Ancient Law *by* ***Henry Maine*** **ISBN:** ***1-59462-128-4*** **$29.95**
The chief object of the following pages is to indicate some of the earliest ideas of mankind, as they are reflected in Ancient Law, and to point out the relation of those ideas to modern thought. *Religiom/History Pages 452*

Far-Away Stories *by* ***William J. Locke*** **ISBN:** ***1-59462-129-2*** **$19.45**
"Good wine needs no bush, but a collection of mixed vintages does. And this book is just such a collection. Some of the stories I do not want to remain buried for ever in the museum files of dead magazine-numbers an author's not unpardonable vanity..." *Fiction Pages 272*

Life of David Crockett *by* ***David Crockett*** **ISBN:** ***1-59462-250-7*** **$27.45**
"Colonel David Crockett was one of the most remarkable men of the times in which he lived. Born in humble life, but gifted with a strong will, an indomitable courage, and unremitting perseverance... *Biographies/New Age Pages 424*

Lip-Reading *by* ***Edward Nitchie*** **ISBN:** ***1-59462-206-X*** **$25.95**
Edward B. Nitchie, founder of the New York School for the Hard of Hearing, now the Nitchie School of Lip-Reading, Inc, wrote "LIP-READING Principles and Practice". The development and perfecting of this meritorious work on lip-reading was an undertaking... *How-to Pages 400*

A Handbook of Suggestive Therapeutics, Applied Hypnotism, Psychic Science **ISBN:** ***1-59462-214-0*** **$24.95**
by ***Henry Munro*** *Health/New Age/Health/Self-help Pages 376*

A Doll's House: and Two Other Plays *by* ***Henrik Ibsen*** **ISBN:** ***1-59462-112-8*** **$19.95**
Henrik Ibsen created this classic when in revolutionary 1848 Rome. Introducing some striking concepts in playwriting for the realist genre, this play has been studied the world over. *Fiction/Classics/Plays 308*

The Light of Asia *by* ***sir Edwin Arnold*** **ISBN:** ***1-59462-204-3*** **$13.95**
In this poetic masterpiece, Edwin Arnold describes the life and teachings of Buddha. The man who was to become known as Buddha to the world was born as Prince Gautama of India but he rejected the worldly riches and abandoned the reigns of power when... *Religion/History/Biographies Pages 170*

The Complete Works of Guy de Maupassant *by* ***Guy de Maupassant*** **ISBN:** ***1-59462-157-8*** **$16.95**
"For days and days, nights and nights, I had dreamed of that first kiss which was to consecrate our engagement, and I knew not on what spot I should put my lips..." *Fiction/Classics Pages 240*

The Art of Cross-Examination *by* ***Francis L. Wellman*** **ISBN:** ***1-59462-309-0*** **$26.95**
Written by a renowned trial lawyer, Wellman imparts his experience and uses case studies to explain how to use psychology to extract desired information through questioning. *How-to/Science/Reference Pages 408*

Answered or Unanswered? *by* ***Louisa Vaughan*** **ISBN:** ***1-59462-248-5*** **$10.95**
Miracles of Faith in China *Religion Pages 112*

The Edinburgh Lectures on Mental Science (1909) *by* ***Thomas*** **ISBN:** ***1-59462-008-3*** **$11.95**
This book contains the substance of a course of lectures recently given by the writer in the Queen Street Hall, Edinburgh. Its purpose is to indicate the Natural Principles governing the relation between Mental Action and Material Conditions... *New Age/Psychology Pages 148*

Ayesha *by* ***H. Rider Haggard*** **ISBN:** ***1-59462-301-5*** **$24.95**
Verily and indeed it is the unexpected that happens! Probably if there was one person upon the earth from whom the Editor of this, and of a certain previous history, did not expect to hear again... *Classics Pages 380*

Ayala's Angel *by* ***Anthony Trollope*** **ISBN:** ***1-59462-352-X*** **$29.95**
The two girls were both pretty, but Lucy who was twenty-one who supposed to be simple and comparatively unattractive, whereas Ayala was credited, as her Bombwhat romantic name might show, with poetic charm and a taste for romance. Ayala when her father died was nineteen... *Fiction Pages 484*

The American Commonwealth *by* ***James Bryce*** **ISBN:** ***1-59462-286-8*** **$34.45**
An interpretation of American democratic political theory. It examines political mechanics and society from the perspective of Scotsman James Bryce *Politics Pages 572*

Stories of the Pilgrims *by* ***Margaret P. Pumphrey*** **ISBN:** ***1-59462-116-0*** **$17.95**
This book explores pilgrims religious oppression in England as well as their escape to Holland and eventual crossing to America on the Mayflower, and their early days in New England... *History Pages 268*

www.bookjungle.com *email: sales@bookjungle.com fax: 630-214-0564 mail: Book Jungle PO Box 2226 Champaign, IL 61825*

Printed in the United Kingdom
by Lightning Source UK Ltd.
136420UK00001B/341/A